Mary Bowen   Liz Hockin

English World

Pupil's Book

5

Unit number and themes Pages	Poster and Unit title	Reading	Grammar	Grammar in conversation
1 Adventure 22	**A journey to adventure**	***Escape from the fire*** text type: the beginning of an adventure story	past continuous / past simple *While Robert was packing his bag, the telephone rang.*	*used to I used to go to my grandmother's house every day.*
2 Adventure 30	**In the mountains**	***Dad's favourite walk*** text type: a personal recount	infinitive of purpose *The family went to Switzerland to have a holiday.*	*have to; had to; will have to I have to take a test. I had to go to school. I will have to study.*
	Revision 1			
3 Engineering 40	**Tunnels and bridges**	***Building for travel*** text type: information, explanation, diagram	present simple passive *This bridge is made of stone. Food is grown by farmers.*	adjectives with *ing, ed I'm interested in sports. Ballet is fascinating.*
4 Engineering 48	**Astonishing structures**	***Great places to visit*** text type: promotional leaflet and review	present perfect + *ever / never Has Ed ever been to Peru? No, he's never been to Peru.*	present perfect + *ever / never Have you ever been abroad? Yes, I've been to England.*
	Revision 2			
5 The ancient world 58	**A story from the ancient world**	***The voyage of Odysseus*** text type: a play	present perfect + *just / yet The ship has just passed the cave. The men have not escaped yet.*	present perfect + *just / yet Have you done your maths yet? I've just finished it.*
6 The ancient world 66	**A legend from the ancient world**	***The Trojan Horse Who is it?*** text type: rhyming poem; acrostic poem	defining relative clauses *They built a horse which / that was made of wood.*	exclamations *The film is so funny! It's such a funny film! They are such good actors!*
	Revision 3			
7 The media 76	**Newspapers**	***Hold the front page!*** text type: information and a newspaper article	present perfect + *for / since She's had a cat for two years. They've had a car since 2005.*	present perfect + *for / since We've lived here for ten years. We've been here since June.*
8 The media 84	**Radio and television**	***News and entertainment*** text type: information and an interview	the definite / indefinite article *Paddy Riley has a chat show. The chat show is entertaining.*	result clauses *The film was so good that I saw it twice.*
	Revision 4			
9 The deep ocean 94	**Deep sea animals**	***Deep sea discovery*** text type: a story with descriptive narative	past simple passive *Molly was fascinated by music. The books were written by him.*	*ought to; want to; need to I ought to revise. I need to study because I want to pass.*
10 The deep ocean 102	**Deep sea exploration**	***The land under the oceans*** text type: information with labelled diagram	second conditional *If they did not have light, the plants would not grow.*	gerunds *I enjoy running. What do you hate doing?*
	Revision 5			
11 Silent heroes 112	**Helping other people**	***Mary Seacole*** text type: biography	reported speech *The doctor said that Mary Seacole was a good nurse.*	reported speech *I said that I didn't like football.*
12 Silent heroes 120	**Saving other people**	***The great race of mercy*** text type: a true life story	countables / uncountables *more, less, fewer; the most, the least, the fewest*	round-up of idiomatic expressions
	Revision 6			

Spelling	Study skills (WB)	Use of English	Class composition / Composition practice (WB)	Listening story
words with *wh* / whistle	alphabetical order; definitions	spelling of adverbs, e.g. *noisy, noisily*	continuing an adventure story	*The skyscraper moneybox* Part 1
words with soft *ch* and hard *ch* / chip, ache	guessing meanings from context; spelling	use of paragraphs	a personal recount	*The skyscraper moneybox* Part 2
suffix *ful* / careful	nouns, dictionary abbreviation, *n.* definitions	adverbs of manner: *carefully*	explanation with a diagram	*The skyscraper moneybox* Part 3
prefix *un* / unhappy	alphabetical order; adjectives, dictionary abbreviation, *adj.*	proper nouns	a review of a visit	*Uncle Bertie goes to the funfair* Part 1
prefix *dis* / disappear	verbs, dictionary abbreviation, *v.* definitions	adverbs of place: *here, inside*	a scene of a play	*Uncle Bertie goes to the funfair* Part 2
suffix *er* / builder	spelling; adverbs, dictionary abbreviation, *adv.*	adverbs of time: *now, yesterday*	an acrostic poem	*Uncle Bertie goes to the funfair* Part 3
compound words / supermarket	making notes	possessive nouns	a newspaper report	*Tim v. Slug* Part 1
words ending *el*	alphabetical order; definitions	possessive adjectives	an interview	*Tim v. Slug* Part 2
words ending *le* / tentacle	making notes	words for reporting direct speech	continuing a story with descriptive narrative	*Tim v. Slug* Part 3
words ending *ey* and *ire*	alphabetical order; spelling	phrases	information from notes and a labelled diagram	*Diamond Quest* Part 1
words with soft *g* / giant	making notes; definitions	possessive pronouns	a biography from notes	*Diamond Quest* Part 2
silent letters, *k, w, b* / knife, wreck, lamb	spelling: alphabetical order	collective nouns	writing a true story from notes and pictures	*Diamond Quest* Part 3

Meet the characters

Let's talk about hobbies!

1 🎧 Look, listen and say.

Computers are great! I play computer games every day.

I read every afternoon. This story is very exciting.

We like music. We sing and play every evening.

Mr Smash

Mrs Swift

Mr Flash   Superboots

A What do they like? Write.

1    She _____

2    He _____

3    They _____

4 How about you? _____

2 Ask and answer.

1

Our favourite sport is basketball. We play three times a week.

Miss Smart   Miss Sparkle

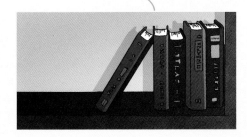

What's his name?

What does he like?

What's he doing now?

How often does he play computer games?

What has he got?

2

3

4

B What are they doing? Write.

1

He _____

2

It _____

3

They _____

4 What are you doing? _____

A **Complete the sentences with the verbs in brackets. Use the past tense.**

1 Mr Smash _____ to the beach. (go)

2 Miss Sparkle and Mr Flash _____ a play. (see)

3 Mrs Swift and Mr Flash _____ Superboots. (visit)

4 They _____ presents for him. (take)

2 Ask and answer.

1

Did he go to the beach?

Yes, he did.   No, he didn't.

2

go – beach?   go – theatre?

have a good time?

3

visit Superboots?   travel by train?

give him presents?

3 Ask and answer.

1

What did she make?

She made a cake.

2

Where – swim?
What – eat?

3

Where – go?
Where – sit?

B Correct the sentences. Use *did not*.

1 Mr Flash made a cake.

2 Miss Sparkle went to the beach.

3 Mr Smash had a bad day.

4 Superboots and Mrs Swift sang a song.

No, he _____

_____

_____

_____

1 🎧 Look and listen.

A Write sentences. Use the past continuous.

 1 Grandpa _____

2 The sun _____

 3 The birds _____

4 What were you doing at this time yesterday? _____

2 Ask and answer.

1

What was she doing?

She was making a pizza.

2  3

4  5

3 Point and make sentences.

While Mr Flash was sailing a boat, Miss Smart was flying a plane.

4 Say and guess the job.

I'm thinking of someone who flies a plane.

You're thinking of a pilot.

B Answer the questions.

1 What is a tourist? A tourist is someone who _____

2 What is an actor? _____

3 What is a farmer? _____

4 What is a pupil? _____

Today we're having a picnic on the beach!

1 🎧 Look and listen.

A Complete the sentences with *much* or *many*.

1 How _____ dolphins are there?

2 How _____ juice is there?

3 They have not got _____ water.

4 They have not got _____ bananas.

2 Ask and answer.

Are there many grapes?

Yes, there are.

Is there much water?

No, there isn't.

1 cakes?	2 sandwiches?
3 fruit?	4 juice?
5 bananas?	6 water?

3 Ask and answer.

How many oranges are there?

There are only a few.

How much juice is there?

There's only a little.

1 bananas?	2 dolphins?
3 water?	4 birds?
5 juice?	6 oranges?

B Complete the sentences with *a few* or *a little*.

1 There is _____ water in the bottle.

2 There are _____ oranges in the basket.

3 I can see _____ birds in the sky.

4 Is there _____ juice in the jug?

Well done, heroes!

1  **Look and listen.**

A **Complete the sentences with *could* and a verb from the box.**

1 The woman _____ not _____ the tree.

2 The little girl _____ not _____ the book.

3 The little boy _____ not _____ quickly.

4 Miss Smart _____ _____ the boy.

run

move

help

reach

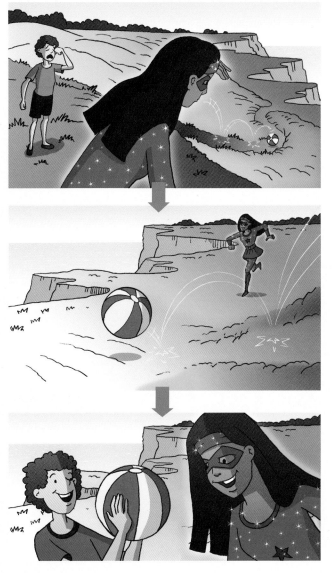

2 Answer the questions.

1 Who was too short?

2 Who was too slow?

3 What was too heavy?

4 Who wasn't tall enough?

5 Who wasn't strong enough?

6 Who wasn't fast enough?

3 Answer the questions.

1 Where was the little girl?

2 Could she reach the high shelf?

3 Why not?

4 Where was the tree?

5 Could the woman lift the tree?

6 Why not?

7 What was the boy doing?

8 Could he get his ball?

9 Why not?

B Complete the sentences with *too* or *enough*.

1 The tree was _____ heavy.

2 The woman was not strong _____ .

3 The little boy was not fast _____ .

4 The shelf was _____ high.

What have we done?

1 🎧 **Look and listen.**

A Complete the sentences with words from the boxes.

| have | has | | cleaned | lost | picked | climbed |

1  Where is my watch? I _____ it.

2  Look! Someone _____ all the apples.

3  The men _____ the mountain.

4 🚗 Look! Nobody _____ the car.

2 Ask and answer.

1

What has she done?

She has made a cake.

2   3

4   5

3 Talk about it.

What should they do now?

B Complete the sentences with *should* and a word from the box.

> wear   go   take   eat

1 Joe is hungry. He _____ something.

2 It's raining. We _____ an umbrella.

3 If you are tired, you _____ to bed.

4 The children _____ their school uniform.

1 🎧 **Look and listen.**

A **Complete the sentences with the correct form of the word in brackets.**

1 Mr Smash was _____ than Miss Smart. (strong)

2 Miss Sparkle was a _____ swimmer than Mr Flash. (good)

3 Miss Smart was a _____ diver than Mr Flash. (bad)

4 Superboots was _____ than Miss Smart. (frightened)

1. Superboots
2. Miss Sparkle
3. Mr Smash
4. Mrs Swift
5. Mr Flash
6. Miss Smart

1. Mrs Swift
2. Miss Sparkle
3. Miss Smart
4. Superboots
5. Mr Flash
6. Mr Smash

2 Answer the questions.

1 Who was the best swimmer?
2 Who was the worst swimmer?
3 Who was the fastest runner?
4 Who was the slowest runner?
5 Who was the strongest hero?
6 Who was the best diver?
7 Who was the bravest hero?
8 Who was the most frightened hero?

3 Answer the questions

1 In the flying competition was Superboots better than Mr Smash?
2 In the swimming competition was Mr Flash worse than Miss Smart?
3 In the flying competition was Miss Sparkle as good as Mrs Swift?

4 Talk about the heroes.

Use these phrases:

faster than	slower than	stronger than
better than	worse than	
braver than	more frightened than	

B Complete the sentences with the correct form of the word in brackets.

1 Mrs Swift was the _____ of all the heroes. (brave)

2 Mr Smash was the _____ . (frightened)

3 Miss Sparkle was the _____ runner in the competition. (good)

4 Superboots was the _____ diver of all the heroes. (bad)

What will we find on this island?

1 🎧 **Look and listen.**

A **Complete the sentences with the verbs in brackets.**
Use the correct forms of the verbs!

1 If they _____ to the north, they _____ to the mountain. (walk, come)

2 If they _____ at the beach, they _____ the sea. (arrive, see)

3 They _____ the lake if they _____ south. (reach, go)

4 Miss Sparkle _____ scared if she _____ a wolf. (be, hear)

2 Answer the questions.

1 If they go north, what will they come to?
2 If they walk south, what will they see?
3 If they go east, what will they come to?
4 If they walk west, what will they arrive at?

3 Ask and answer.

What might they see on the mountain?

They might see an eagle.

What else might they see?

1 see – lake?
2 see – forest?
3 hear – forest?
4 see – beach?
5 do – beach?

B Complete the sentences. Use *might* + verb. Use your own ideas.

1 Look at those dark clouds. It _____

2 There are animals in the forest. We _____

3 I've got some money. I _____

4 It's Emily's birthday next week. She _____

A journey to adventure

Reading 🔊 **Escape from the fire**

Chapter 1: Grandad

Robert was excited. He was going to stay with his grandfather at the weekend. Lucy, his cousin, was going to stay too. She was the same age as Robert and they were good friends.

While Robert was packing his bag, the telephone rang noisily. Robert answered it. It was Lucy.

"I hope we have a great weekend," said Lucy.

"So do I," said Robert. "It's always good fun at Grandad's."

While Robert was travelling on the bus, he thought about Grandad. There were two things about him that Robert and Lucy really liked. First, he was very, very clever. He was an inventor. He invented lots of things, but mostly he invented new kinds of mobile phones. The other thing they liked was that Grandad loved history. His house was full of history books. When Robert and Lucy came to stay, Grandad told them exciting stories from history. The cousins loved the stories because they were true. They loved Grandad's tales of explorers who used to sail across the oceans and travel across deserts to distant lands.

Robert knocked on Grandad's door. Mrs Green, the maid, opened it.

"Hello, Robert," she said. "Come in."

"Hello, Mrs Green," Robert said. "How are you?"

"I'm fine," said Mrs Green. She took his bag from him. "Your grandfather is in his study."

Robert hurried into Grandad's study. "Hello, Grandad," he began. Then he stopped in surprise.

Grandad was sitting in an armchair. There was a big bandage on his foot.

"Grandad, what happened?" Robert asked.

"I've hurt my ankle," Grandad said. "The doctor says I mustn't walk on it for a few days."

"Poor Grandad. Does it hurt? I'll help you and so will Lucy. Where is she? Has she arrived yet?"

Grandad looked worried. "I'm not sure," he said. "I think she has disappeared."

"Disappeared?" said Robert. "What do you mean?"

Grandad leaned towards him and whispered, "I think she has travelled back in time."

Chapter 2: The time-travel phones

Robert looked at Grandad, amazed. "How could Lucy have travelled back in time?" he asked.

Grandad showed him a mobile phone. "Look at this," he said. "This is not an ordinary phone. This is my newest invention."

Robert thought the mobile phone looked ordinary. "What's special about it?" he asked.

"Do you promise not to tell anyone?"

"Not even Lucy?"

"Lucy knows already."

"Not even Mum and Dad?"

"I'll tell them soon."

"Okay. So what does it do?" asked Robert.

"With this mobile phone you can travel back in time."

"Wow!" Robert exclaimed. "Can you really do that?"

Grandad nodded proudly. "I've worked on this invention for two years," he said. "It's ready now."

Robert's eyes widened. "How does it work?"

"Let me show you. You put in the date you want to visit. Then you put in the place you want to visit. Then you put in the password, *Adventure*."

"Did you tell Lucy this?"

"Yes. And now one of the time-travel phones is missing."

"How many time-travel phones have you made?" Robert asked.

"Four," Grandad shook his head. "I'm worried, Robert. I think Lucy has used the missing phone to travel back in time."

"Wow!" Robert exclaimed. "Where do you think she has gone?"

From *Escape from the Fire*, by Richard Brown (Macmillan English Explorers Level 4)

Reading comprehension and vocabulary

1 **Who said these words? Circle the answer.**

1 I hope we have a great weekend.	Lucy	Robert
2 It's always good fun at Grandad's.	Lucy	Robert
3 Hello, Robert. Come in.	grandfather	Mrs Green
4 I've hurt my ankle.	grandfather	Mrs Green
5 What's special about it?	Robert	grandfather
6 You put in the date you want to visit.	Robert	grandfather

2 **Talk about the answers to these questions.**

1 Do you think Grandad is an interesting person? Why or why not?

2 Do you think time travel could be good fun or too dangerous? Why?

3 Look at the title of the story again. Do you know about any big fires? Where might Lucy have gone?

3 **Label the picture.**   maid   study   inventor   armchair   ankle   bandage

1 _____ 2 _____ 3 _____ 4 _____ 5 _____ 6 _____

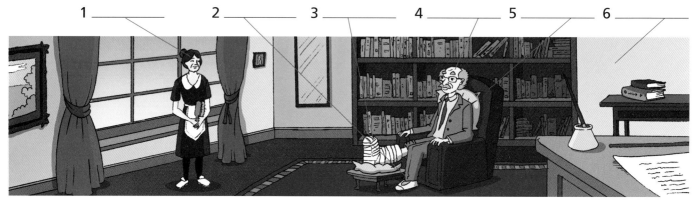

4 **Match the verbs and the definitions.**

a nod   b escape   c shake   d promise   e mean

1 to say you will do something   _____

2 to move an object from side to side quickly   _____

3 to move your head up and down   _____

4 to explain an idea   _____

5 to get away from   _____

Hi! It's time for some fantastic grammar!

1 **Look and read.**

Robert was packing his bag.
The telephone rang.

While Robert was packing his bag, the telephone rang.

2 **Look, read and match. Write the letters.**

a   b   c   d

1 While the boys were playing football, a dog took their ball. _____

2 While Jim was swimming, he saw a shark. _____

3 While we were having a picnic, it started to rain. _____

4 While Sue was watching TV, someone knocked on the door. _____

3 **Complete the sentences. The pictures will help you.**

Hello.

1 While Meg was shopping,
   she ...

2 While the children were
   walking in the forest, they ...

3 ... , he found a ring.

4 ... , the telephone rang.

1 🎧 **Listen and read.**

Molly:	Do you remember when you were little?
Sam:	Yes, of course. I used to go to my grandmother's house every day.
Molly:	Really? Why?
Sam:	Because she used to look after me while Mum was at work.
Molly:	Did you like going to her house?
Sam:	It was great. Grandma used to read stories and sing songs. And we used to make cakes together, too.
Molly:	That sounds nice.
Sam:	Yes, it was.

2 **Think, write and say.**

Think about when you were little. What happened then but not now?

I used to build castles with bricks.

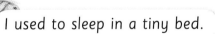
I used to play with dolls.

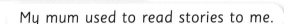
I used to sleep in a tiny bed.

My mum used to read stories to me.

3 **Let's talk!**

Tell me about when you were little.

When I was little, I used to ...

Useful phrases

How about you?   Really?

Why?   That sounds nice.

In words with *wh*, sometimes you can't hear the *h*.

Wh**ere**
Where will the time machine take me?

1 **Complete the words with *wh*. Write the words. Read the words.**

 ____eel

_____

 ____isper

_____

 ____ale

_____

 ____istle

_____

🎧 **Listen and say the words.**

2 **Complete these question words with *wh*. Write the words. Read the words.**

____ere   ____y   ____at   ____en   ____ich

_____   _____   _____   _____   _____

🎧 **Listen and say the words.**

3 **Choose a word from Activity 2 to complete these questions.**

1 Hello, _____ is your name?

2 _____ will the train arrive?

3 _____ shoes do you like?

4 _____ is your homework, Dan?

5 _____ does an elephant have a long trunk?

4 🎧 **Listen and say.**

Time machine, time machine, take me away!
Take me somewhere exciting today!

Show me the world of long ago
When mammoths walked through ice and snow.
Show me the pyramids rising high
Into the Ancient Egyptian sky.
Show me adventurers brave and bold
Sailing the seas for Aztec gold.

Time machine, time machine, take me away!
Take me somewhere exciting today!

Class composition

Do you remember Grandad's invention?
Here is the start of another adventure!

1 **Look at the pictures.**

Read the speech bubbles.

2 **Write the story.**

The Chinese inventors

Grandad was holding the time-travel phone. He put in 'China, 2000 years ago, Adventure'.
Suddenly, they were standing in a large courtyard.

Those soldiers look very fierce.

Chinese ladies always used to carry umbrellas in the garden.

These men are scientists and I think they are inventing ...

... gunpowder!

Look out! The soldiers are coming!

1 **Look and read.** **2**  **Look, listen and read.** **3** **Talk about the story.**

The skyscraper moneybox – Part 1

In the mountains

Dad's favourite walk

My dad used to live in Switzerland and he worked as a mountain guide. This summer Dad wanted to visit Switzerland again. In July I travelled to the mountains with Mum, Dad and my twin brother Fred. We stayed in a hotel in a little village and we had a great time.

One day Dad took us on his favourite walk. First, we followed a narrow path through a meadow. There were lots of flowers and there were goats with bells round their necks. They tinkled when the goats moved. After that, the path went through a forest. It was shady and quiet. It reminded me of Red Riding Hood but I didn't see a wolf! After the forest, the path climbed steeply towards the mountain peaks. It led between huge rocks and then the walk became a real adventure. Dad had some surprises for us.

We walked into a deep, narrow ravine. We could hear the river splashing over the rocks at the bottom. While we were walking, we heard a distant roar. Gradually, it got louder. We walked round a massive boulder and there was the most amazing sight. Water was falling straight down the mountain and crashing onto the rocks below us.

The sound was incredible. A waterfall really does roar. It sounded like an angry beast. We couldn't hear each other at all. Dad beckoned to us and we followed him. The path led behind the waterfall. It was amazing. On the left of the path was the mountainside and on the right was falling water. I thought it was fantastic but it was a bit scary, too. It was quite dark and very noisy.

The path came out from behind the waterfall but round the corner it stopped at the edge of a high cliff. There was a short wooden bridge with rope at the sides and it was swinging in the breeze. It looked terrifying but Dad knew it was safe. Anyway, it was the only way to cross the ravine. The bridge swung even more when we walked on it. We walked slowly to keep steady. Fred and I thought it was fun but Dad had to help Mum. She is frightened of high places. She walked with her eyes shut!

We sat on the rocks and ate our lunch. Then we set off again. We climbed higher and higher. After an hour our legs were aching but at last we came to the best place on the whole mountain. It was a huge glacier and it looked like a frozen river of ice. There were lots of other people there too. There was a cave in the ice. There were rooms in the cave and ice furniture. Fred sat on the ice chair and played the ice piano. It was funny!

The last surprise of all was a ride down to the hotel on the little mountain train. We were exhausted but it was a brilliant walk.

Reading comprehension and vocabulary

1 Answer the questions.

1 Who used to live in Switzerland?
2 When did Susan and her family travel to the mountains?
3 Which story did Susan think of in the forest?
4 What did the waterfall sound like?
5 Who did not like the bridge? Why not?
6 What was special about the glacier?
7 Why did Susan laugh inside the ice cave?
8 How did Susan feel at the end of the day?

2 Think about the answers to these questions.

1 Why do you think the forest reminded Susan of Red Riding Hood?
2 Why did Mum shut her eyes when she walked across the bridge?
3 Which part of the walk do you think Susan liked best? Why?
4 Which part do you think was the best? Why?

3 Match the adjectives and the definitions. Write the word.

> exhausted   massive   deep   shady   incredible

1 full of shadows _____
2 going a long way down _____
3 very big _____
4 not believable _____
5 very tired _____

4 Match an adjective from Activity 3 to each noun below.
Write phrases.

> ravine   children   boulder   forest   sound

_____   _____

_____   _____

_____

Unit 2 Reading comprehension and vocabulary: literal and deductive questions; definitions; phrase

Grammar

Hello, my dears! It's time for some more grammar.

1 Look and read.

The family went to Switzerland to have a holiday.
They walked up a steep path to reach the waterfall.
To get past the waterfall they walked behind the water.

2 Finish the sentences. Write the letters.

1 They walked through a meadow and a forest ...	A to eat their lunch.
2 To reach the other side of the ravine ...	B they took a little mountain train.
3 They walked slowly ...	C to reach the path to the waterfall.
4 They sat on some rocks ...	D they crossed a wooden bridge.
5 They climbed high into the mountains ...	E to keep steady.
6 To get down to the village ...	F to see the glacier.

1 _____   2 _____   3 _____   4 _____   5 _____   6 _____

3 Ask and answer. The words in the boxes can help you.

Why do you go to school?

We go to school to learn.

1 Why do you do sports?
2 Why do you go shopping?
3 Why do you go to the cinema?
4 Why do you have holidays?
5 Why do you have mobiles?
6 Why do you wear glasses?

speak to our friends

see better

see films

rest and have fun

keep fit and strong

buy things

Grammar in conversation

1 🎧 **Listen and read.**

Daisy: Oh dear…

Ken: What's the matter? You look worried.

Daisy: I'm feeling nervous.

Ken: Why?

Daisy: I have to take my Science exam today.

Ken: Really?

Daisy: I had to study for hours last night.

Ken: Poor you!

Daisy: I'm sure I won't pass.

Ken: It'll be fine.

Daisy: If I fail, I'll have to take it again next month.

Ken: Don't worry! Just keep calm.

Daisy: Oh dear…

2 Think, write and say.

I have to take a test.

What do you have to do today?

I had to write a composition.

What did you have to do yesterday?

I'll have to finish my project.

What will you have to do tomorrow?

These words and pictures can help you:

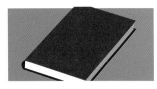   

Science   Maths   English   Art   History   Music

3 Let's talk!

Talk about today, yesterday and tomorrow.

Useful phrases

Oh dear…   Really?

Why?

Poor you!   Don't worry!

Spelling

In some words the letters *ch* make a soft sound.
In some words the letters *ch* make a hard sound like *k*.

---

lun**ch**   We sat on the rocks to eat our lunch.

a**ch**ing   After an hour our legs were aching.

---

1 Complete these words with *ch*. Write the words. Read the words.

lun____   bun____   mun____   cat____   ____op   ____ip

_____   _____   _____   _____   _____   _____

🎧 **Listen and say the words.**

2 Complete these words with *ch*. Write the words. Read the words.

an____or   s____ool   stoma____   a____e   heada____e   tootha____e

_____   _____   _____   _____   _____   _____

🎧 **Listen and say the words.**

3 Complete this text. Use words from Activities 1 and 2.

Mum was putting a _____ of flowers in a vase when Ben

came home from _____ .

"Ben," said Mum. "You don't look well today.

Have you got a _____ ?"

"No, it's not my head," said Ben. "It's my tooth. I've got _____ ."

"I'll take you to the dentist," said Mum. "We will go after _____ ."

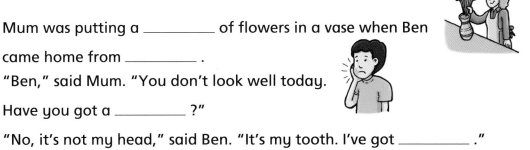

4 🎧 **Listen and say.**

Munch, munch, munch
On a bunch, bunch, bunch.
Munch on a bunch of bananas for lunch.

Fred wrote about the holiday in the mountains, too.

1 Read.

When Susan, Fred, Mum and Dad were in Switzerland, they went to a lake. Afterwards, Fred drew pictures and wrote about their day. Look at his pictures and Dad's photo of the lake. Read Fred's captions.

We went to the lake by train.

We swam in the lake. It was freezing! We went across the lake by boat.

We all ate ice creams. I had chocolate and lemon.   The train to our village was crowded.

2 Write Fred's recount of the day. Use the pictures and the captions to help you.

One day we went to a very big lake. We went by _____

_____

1 Look and read.   **2** 🎧 Look, listen and read.   **3** Talk about the story.

The skyscraper moneybox – Part 2

At school the next day there was a new boy in class.

Jamie, can you look after Tim today?

This is where we have Science.

Do you want to play football?

Sorry, Tim. They're very rude.

After school...

Why aren't you going home, Tim?

Do you want to come to my house?

Would you like a sandwich, Tim?

Ha ha ha!

See you tomorrow.

It's too light.

Someone's stolen my money!

And I think I know who the thief is...

Revision 1

Listening

1 Talk about the pictures. Read and match. Write the letters in the boxes.

A The men who arrived at the museum in a fast black car

B The helicopter pilot

C The two children, Ben and Sue

D The tall man who was on the roof of the museum

E The man with the camera

F The firemen

2 🎧 Listen. Who is speaking? Write the letter.

1 ___   2 ___   3 ___   4 ___   5 ___   6 ___

3 🎧 Listen again. Listen for these words.

roof   luck   fast   theatre   camera   ladder

4 Choose one of the characters in the story. Imagine you are that character. Tell the story from your character's point of view.

> When Ben and I were sitting by the river, we saw a car. It was going really fast over the bridge and . . .

Now you can do the project on page 130

3 Tunnels and bridges

Building for travel

Tunnels

People cross mountains by car or train and they cross water by boat but these journeys take time. Tunnels can go under mountains and under water. They make journeys much quicker.

The longest road tunnel in the world is in Norway. It is 24.5 km long.

A tunnel is an enormous tube and a tube is a very strong shape. When engineers build a tunnel, they make a tube shape in the ground. If the tunnel is not deep the work is easier. Engineers use two cut and cover methods.

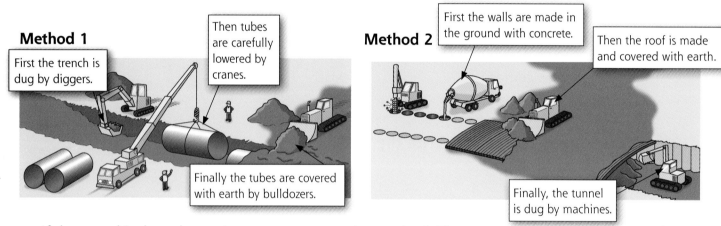

Method 1

First the trench is dug by diggers.

Then tubes are carefully lowered by cranes.

Finally the tubes are covered with earth by bulldozers.

Method 2

First the walls are made in the ground with concrete.

Then the roof is made and covered with earth.

Finally, the tunnel is dug by machines.

If the tunnel is deep the engineers must use another method. They use an enormous machine to bore into the earth and rock. It is called a Tunnel Boring Machine (TBM). It cuts rock and clears it away at the same time. It can cut and clear a 25–30 metre length of tunnel each day.

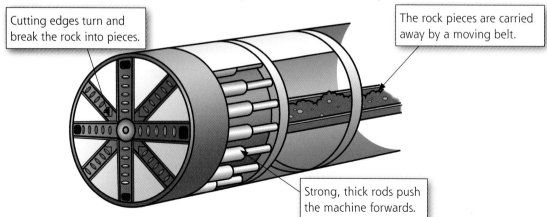

Cutting edges turn and break the rock into pieces.

The rock pieces are carried away by a moving belt.

Strong, thick rods push the machine forwards.

The Channel Tunnel joins England and France. It is a railway tunnel and it goes under the sea. Engineers used four TBMs at the same time to cut the tunnel.

Bridges

People have built bridges across rivers for thousands of years. There are many different kinds of bridge.

Beam bridge

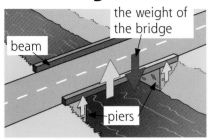

Piers support the weight of the bridge.

The beam bridge is the simplest kind of bridge. A log or a plank across a stream is a short beam bridge. A long beam bridge is supported by piers at each end. This kind of bridge cannot cross a very wide river.

Arch bridge

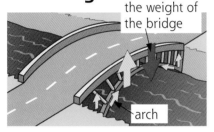

The shape of the arch helps to support a longer, heavier bridge.

An arch can support a lot of weight so it can hold up a longer bridge. Some bridges are made of more than one arch. Bridges made by people long ago often had many arches.

The Bridge of 33 Arches in Iran is four hundred years old. This fascinating bridge has arches on two levels. In summer, it is full of visitors and delighted children paddle in the shallow water underneath.

Suspension bridge

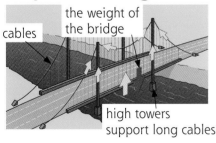

Strong cables can support a very long bridge.

This kind of bridge can be even longer. The bridge is supported by strong cables. The cables are supported by tall towers. Suspension bridges are designed by engineers to cross wide rivers and sea channels.

Reading comprehension and vocabulary

1 Read and write *true* or *false*.

1 The longest road tunnel in the world is in Norway. _____

2 If the tunnel is not deep the work is more difficult. _____

3 The tunnel boring machine cuts 25–30 metres of rock each hour. _____

4 The Channel Tunnel joins England and Paris. _____

5 A long beam bridge is supported by a pier in the middle. _____

6 An arch bridge can hold up a longer bridge than a beam bridge. _____

7 Suspension bridges are designed by engine drivers. _____

8 A suspension bridge can cross wide rivers and sea channels. _____

2 Talk about the answers to these questions.

1 What bridges and tunnels do you know? Make a list.

Which is your favourite bridge? Why?

2 Which journey do you think is better:

a a four hour car journey through the mountains?

b a one hour car journey through a tunnel?

Why?

3 Which do you like better:

a the old Bridge of 33 Arches?   b the modern suspension bridge?

Why?

3 Write the words on the correct lines.

labels   caption   diagram

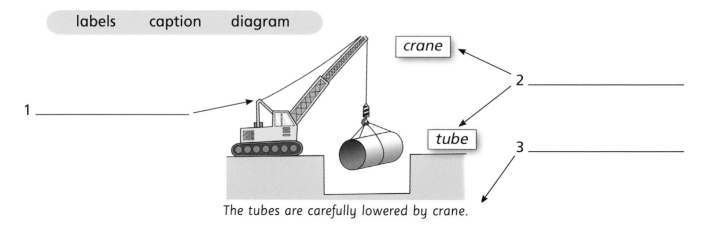

The tubes are carefully lowered by crane.

Unit 3 Reading comprehension and vocabulary: true/false; personal response; diagram vocabulary

Grammar

1 Look and read.

It's grammar time again!

This bridge is made of stone.
Small bridges are built across streams.
Large bridges are designed by engineers.

2 Finish the sentences. Write the letters.

1 This is how a tunnel …
2 First a trench is dug …
3 Next huge tubes are lowered …
4 Finally the tubes are covered with earth …
5 Sometimes deep tunnels are built …
6 Enormous machines are used …

A … by bulldozers.
B … through mountains.
C … is built.
D … into the trench by cranes.
E … to cut into the earth and rock.
F … by diggers.

1 _____ 2 _____ 3 _____ 4 _____ 5 _____ 6 _____

3 Ask and answer. The words in the box can help you.

Where are tunnels built?

Tunnels are built through mountains.

1 Where – bridges – built?
2 Who – bridges – designed by?
3 What – a crane – used for?
4 Who – planes – flown by?
5 Who – food – grown by?
6 Where – bread – made?

in a bakery

by pilots

for lifting things

across rivers

by farmers

by engineers

Grammar in conversation

1 🎧 Listen and read.

Molly: What are your hobbies, Sam?

Sam: Well, I'm very interested in collecting stamps.

Molly: Really? Isn't that rather boring?

Sam: I don't get bored by it.

Molly: I don't find stamps very interesting, I'm afraid.

Sam: Nonsense! Take a look at these.
They're fascinating.

Molly: Hmm …You may be fascinated by them, Sam.
I prefer a more exciting hobby.

Sam: Such as?

Molly: Pop music!

Sam: Oh! How boring!

2 Think, write and say.

What are your hobbies?

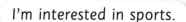
I'm interested in sports.

Ballet is fascinating.

What activities don't you like?

I think computer games are very boring.

I don't find football very interesting, I'm afraid.

3 Let's talk!

What are your hobbies?

I'm very interested in reading.

Useful phrases

Well …

Really?

… I'm afraid.

Nonsense!

I prefer …

Spelling

We can add *full* to the end of some words to make adjectives. When we add *full* to a word, we drop the final *l*.

care + full ➡ **care**ful
Be careful when you cross the road.

1 Add *ful* to these words. Write the words. Read the words.

wonder _____   care _____   watch _____   play _____   use _____   help _____

_____ _____ _____ _____ _____ _____

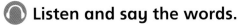 Listen and say the words.

Be careful when you spell this word.

beauty + full ➡ **beauti**ful

If the noun ends with consonant + y, we change the y to i then add ful.

2 Complete the sentences with words from Activity 1.

1 An object that you use often is _____.

2 A person, place or thing that has beauty is _____.

3 A person or animal that enjoys fun and games is _____.

4 A person, place or object that you think is really good is _____.

5 A person or animal that watches carefully is _____.

6 A person who helps a lot is _____.

7 A person who takes care in doing things is _____.

3 Listen and sing.

London Bridge is falling down,
Falling down, falling down.
London Bridge is falling down,
My fair lady.
Build it up with wood and clay…
Wood and clay will wash away…
Build it up with stones so strong
Stones so strong, stones so strong.
It will last for ages long,
My fair lady.

What facts can you find about the Channel Tunnel? How does it work?

1 **Look at the photographs and the diagram. Read the labels and captions.**

London to Paris travel time by train: 2½ hours.

The Channel Tunnel joins England and France. Total length: 50.450 km; under the sea: 38 km

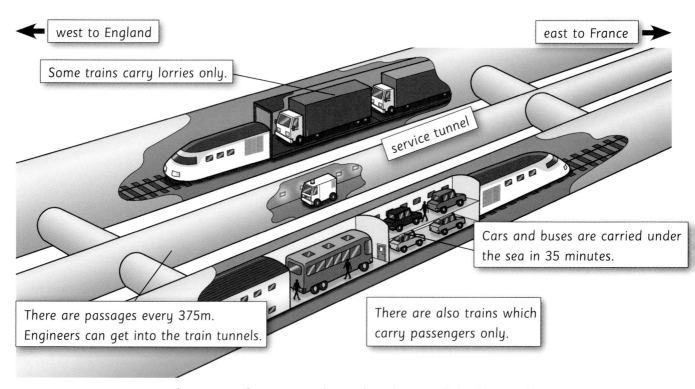

west to England

east to France

Some trains carry lorries only.

service tunnel

Cars and buses are carried under the sea in 35 minutes.

There are passages every 375m. Engineers can get into the train tunnels.

There are also trains which carry passengers only.

There are three tunnels under the English Channel.

2 **Write two paragraphs about the Channel Tunnel.**

Paragraph 1: Write information about the tunnel.

Paragraph 2: Explain how the tunnel works.

1 Look and read.   2 🎧 Look, listen and read.   3 Talk about the story.

The skyscraper moneybox – Part 3

Reading  **Great places to visit**

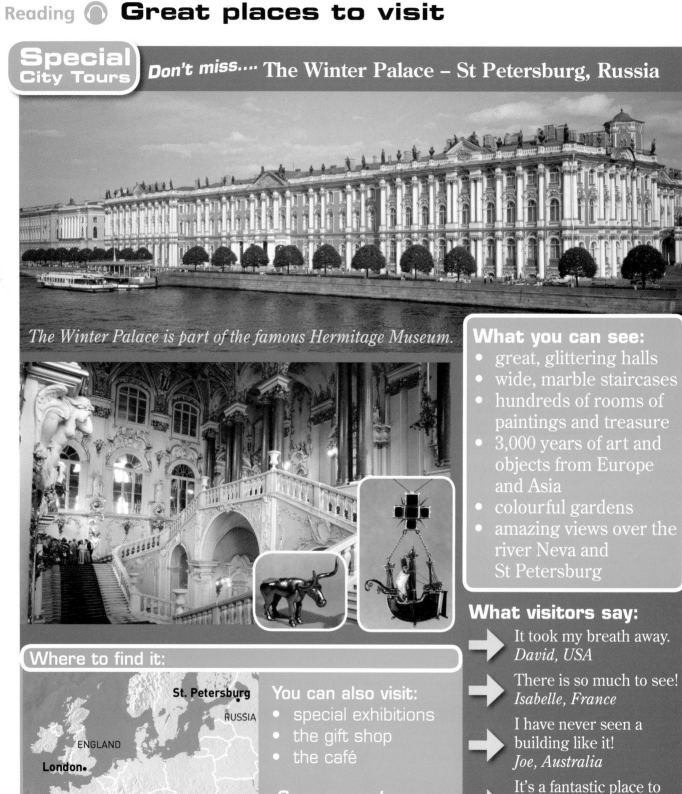

Special City Tours

Don't miss.... **The Winter Palace – St Petersburg, Russia**

The Winter Palace is part of the famous Hermitage Museum.

What you can see:
• great, glittering halls
• wide, marble staircases
• hundreds of rooms of paintings and treasure
• 3,000 years of art and objects from Europe and Asia
• colourful gardens
• amazing views over the river Neva and St Petersburg

What visitors say:

It took my breath away. *David, USA*

There is so much to see! *Isabelle, France*

I have never seen a building like it! *Joe, Australia*

It's a fantastic place to visit! *Masha, Russia*

Where to find it:

St. Petersburg
RUSSIA
ENGLAND
London.

You can also visit:
• special exhibitions
• the gift shop
• the café

Open every day except Monday

The Winter Palace – online reviews

When I first saw the Winter Palace, I couldn't believe my eyes. It is huge and it seems to go on for ever. I really liked the green walls and the tall white columns with gold at the top. There are even statues on the roof. It looks like a big sugary cake!

You must go inside the palace because it is stunning. There is marble and gold everywhere, with huge chandeliers hanging from the ceilings. The lights make everything look shiny and new. It's amazing to think that for two hundred years people lived in it all the time. Now the Winter Palace is full of treasures from the past. Every room has something wonderful.

I really enjoyed my visit. Here are two tips for other visitors:

1 Wear comfortable shoes because you have to walk a lot.

2 Go in the morning, because there are long queues in the afternoon.

Luke, Canada

I wanted to see everything in the Winter Palace but you can't see everything in one day. There were rooms full of paintings but I liked the precious objects the best.

In one room there's a shiny gold bull from the tomb of a nomadic chief. It's hard to believe that it is more than 4,000 years old. It is unusual because there is a hole in its back. When the archaeologists opened the tomb they found four bulls. There was a silver rod in the back of each bull. The rods held a canopy over the body of the chief.

We're going to London with Special City tours next week. We're going on the London Eye. A ride on this huge wheel is called a flight. I hope it's good! It sounds really exciting in the leaflet.

After that we're going to the pyramids at Giza. We're going to go inside the great pyramid to the king's chamber. I think Special City Tours are great!

Carla, Spain

Special City Tours

Don't miss... The London Eye – London, England

What you can do:

- take a 30 minute flight on the tallest wheel in the world
- rise up in a glass pod to 135 metres above the ground
- study the engineering of this amazing structure

What you can see:

- famous London buildings, bridges, the river Thames
- 40 km across England on a clear day

Reading comprehension and vocabulary

1 Choose the correct answer.

1 The Winter Palace is on the river _____.

   a Petersburg **b** Neva **c** Russia

2 The staircases are made of _____.

   a gold **b** wood **c** marble

3 The palace contains art and culture from Europe and _____.

   a Asia **b** America **c** Africa

4 Archaeologists found a gold bull in the _____ of a chief.

   a tunnel **b** canopy **c** tomb

5 Carla is going to go into the king's _____ in the great pyramid.

   a hall **b** chamber **c** palace

6 You can see 40 kilometres across _____ on the London Eye.

   a England **b** London **c** the river Thames

2 Talk about the answers to these questions.

1 Why do you think there are long queues at the Winter Palace in the afternoon?
2 Why do you think you can't see everything at the Winter Palace in one day?
3 Why do you think Carla found it hard to believe that the bull was more than 4,000 years old?
4 Do you like old buildings? Why or why not?

3 Name the objects.

gift shop   canopy   staircase   chandelier   column   leaflet

Grammar

Guess what! It's grammar again!

1 Look and read.

Ed Darcy is a famous explorer.
He has visited many countries in the world.
Has he ever been to Africa?
Yes, he's been to Africa.
Has he ever been to China?
No, he's never been to China.

2 Ask and answer.

Ed's Visits

South America ✓   China ✗
Peru ✗   The Arctic ✓
North America ✓   The Antarctic ✗
Canada ✗   Russia ✗
Africa ✓   Australia ✓
Egypt ✓

Has Ed ever been to South America?

Yes, he's been to South America.

Has he ever been to Peru?

No, he's never been to Peru.

1 Africa   2 North America   3 Russia   4 The Arctic   5 Canada   6 China   7 Australia

8 The Antarctic   9 Egypt

3 Ed always wears the same boots. Ask and answer.

Have Ed's boots been to China?

No, they've never been to China.

Have they been to the Arctic?

Yes, they've been to the Arctic.

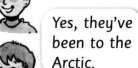

1 Australia   2 Russia   3 Africa   4 The Antarctic   5 South America   6 Egypt   7 Peru   8 Canada

1 🎧 Listen and read.

Ken:	Have you travelled much, Daisy?
Daisy:	Yes, a bit.
Ken:	Have you ever been abroad?
Daisy:	Yes, I have.
Ken:	Where have you been?
Daisy:	I've been to England, Spain and America.
Ken:	Wow! Lucky you! Have you ever been to Africa?
Daisy:	No, I've never been there.
	How about you? Have you travelled much?
Ken:	No, not much. And I've never been abroad.
Daisy:	Never mind. You'll go one day.

2 Think, write and say.

Which countries have you been to? Which towns or cities have you visited?

I've been to America.
I've visited New York.

I've been to Russia.
I've visited St Petersburg.

Which places would you like to visit?

I'd like to go to Dubai.
I've never been there.

I've never been to America.
I'd like to go to there.

3 Let's talk!

Have you travelled much?

Yes, a bit.

Useful phrases
abroad
Lucky you!
Wow!
Never mind!

Spelling

We can add un to the beginning of some words.
We make a new word with the opposite meaning.

---

usual ➡ unusual

It is unusual because there is a hole in its back.

1 **Add *un* to these adjectives to make opposites. Write the words.**

___kind   ___ happy   ___ true   ___ friendly   ___ usual

_____ _____ _____ _____ _____

🎧 **Listen and say the words.**

2 **Use words from Activity 1 to complete the sentences.**

1 Dan was _____ because he couldn't do his homework.

2 Mr Brown never says hello to us. He is very _____.

3 You must never be _____ to little children.

4 The story of *Jack and the Beanstalk* is _____. It did not really happen.

5 This bird is _____ because it makes its nest under the ground.

3 **Add *un* to these verbs to make opposites. Write the words.**

___ wrap   ___ do   ___ cover   ___fold

_____ _____ _____ _____

🎧 **Listen and say the words.**

4 🎧 **Listen and say.**

I've never crossed a desert
In the burning sun.
I've never watched the Northern Lights
Hanging in the sky.
I've never climbed a mountain
To its snowy top.
I've never seen an eagle
Or heard its lonely cry.
I've never swum with dolphins

In the clear blue sea.
But one day I will, I will,
I will – just wait and see!

Class composition

Imagine you visited the pyramids at Giza!

1 Read the leaflet.

Special City Tours *Don't miss....* The Pyramids – Giza, Egypt

The tallest pyramid is 138.8 m high

steep and narrow steps

Hold on tight!

Where to find the pyramids:

Giza•Cairo

EGYPT

4,500 years old! It was in the sand next to the great pyramid

What you can see
- the three great pyramids
- the smaller queens' pyramids
- a king's boat

What you can do
- go inside the Great Pyramid to the king's chamber
- walk all round the king's boat in the museum
- ride on a camel

What visitors say:

➡ Everyone should go to the pyramids – they're fantastic!

➡ The pyramids are huge. The ancient Egyptians were amazing engineers.

➡ The boat is wonderful – it doesn't look old at all.

➡ Ride on a camel, it's fun but be careful when it gets up!

➡ You'll enjoy everything at Giza. We had a great day out.

2 Imagine you

- went in the Great Pyramid   • saw the king's boat   • rode on a camel.

Write a review of your visit.

1 Look and read.   2 🎧 Look, listen and read.   3 Talk about the story.

Uncle Bertie goes to the funfair – Part 1

Revision 2

1 🎧 **Listen and read.**   **2** **Talk about the castle.**   **3** **Read again.**

A castle in Scotland

Have you ever been to a castle? If you visit this old castle in Scotland you will find lots of surprises.

A fascinating ruin

The castle is a ruin. Stones have fallen from the walls and the roof has disappeared. Nobody lives in it now but a long time ago, Scottish kings lived here and the castle used to be full of people. There were soldiers and horses, maids and servants. Many powerful men lived and worked in the castle. Many important people visited it. Five tall, square towers stood inside the castle walls. There were big guns inside the towers. Soldiers fired the guns and they kept the castle safe.

Tunnels under the walls

Four hundred and fifty years ago an army attacked the castle. The walls were high and strong and they could not get inside. They dug a deep, wide tunnel under the castle walls. The soldiers inside the castle heard the noise. They dug another tunnel and caught the attackers underground. If you visit the castle you will see the tunnels. You can climb down the tunnels but you have to go carefully. They are lit but the floors are rough and rocky.

A room under the ground

When the soldiers caught somebody they put him in a room deep under the ground. If you visit the castle, you will see this room, too. It is shaped like a bottle. The walls are made of rock. Nobody has ever climbed them. There is a small opening in the roof, like the top of a bottle. It is the only way in. There are no windows. Once a person was in the room, he could not get out. People are not put in here now, of course, but visitors can easily imagine what is was like inside – cold, dark and very, very scary!

Listening

1 **Talk about the pictures. They are in the wrong order. Can you make a story from them?**

A

B

C

Open the doors! D

E

F

2 🎧 **Listen to the story. Point to the pictures.**

3 🎧 **Listen again. Write the letters.**

1 ____   2 ____   3 ____   4 ____   5 ____   6 ____

4 🎧 **Listen again. Fill in the gaps.**

The old stone castle was _____. It stood on an island with _____ all around it. The castle was _____ but the people who lived there were not _____. A year ago their _____ left the castle to fight a battle in a _____ far away. He never returned. One day a boy was standing at the top of one of the _____. In the distance he could see a great _____. Soldiers were coming to the castle! The people were very _____. Quickly they closed the huge _____ doors. The _____ arrived at the castle and stopped at the _____ bridge. "Open the doors!" shouted a _____. "Do not be frightened!" The people _____ the castle knew that voice. It was the prince! The prince was back and the people were happy _____.

5 **Cover the text in Activity 4 above. Tell the story in your own words.**

Now you can do the project on page 131

5 A story from the ancient world

Reading 🎧

Odysseus was a famous Greek hero. He lived in Greece but for many years he was away from his wife and his son. He was fighting in a long war. At last the war ended and Odysseus began his voyage home. On the way he met many strange creatures.

The voyage of Odysseus

Scene 1

Setting: on Odysseus' ship near rocky cliffs

Characters: Odysseus; the sea captain; sailors; a monster with six heads

Odysseus:	Listen, men. There are two horrifying sea monsters nearby. The first one has twelve legs, six necks and six heads, with three sets of teeth in each one!
Captain:	That's awful! We have never seen such a terrifying creature!
Odysseus:	If a ship sails too near, the monster will …
Sailors:	Help! The ship is rocking!
Odysseus:	Row, row as fast as you can! The monster lives in the cave under those cliffs. He may be sleeping now but I will fight him if I have to.
Sailors:	Row! Row!
Captain:	We have just passed the cave. We are safe!
Sailor 1:	No! Look at the water! We haven't escaped yet.
Sailor 2:	The ship is spinning round and round. What is happening?
Odysseus:	It is the other monster! It is a giant whirlpool. It will pull us under the sea!
Sailors:	We must row!
Monster:	Grrr!

Sailor 1:	What is that?
Captain:	It's a giant dog!
Odysseus:	No, it is the monster with six heads!
Sailor 2:	Look, it is rising out of the water!
Monster:	Grrr!
Sailor 1:	Help! It is attacking us.
Captain:	It is grabbing the sailors. It is eating them! Row! Row!
Odysseus:	Now a storm is coming! The waves are getting higher and higher.
Captain:	The wind is tearing the sail.
Sailor 2:	The mast has broken!
Captain:	The ship is turning over! Help! Help!

Scene 2

Setting: on the beach of a small island

Characters: Odysseus; Calypso (a girl)

Odysseus:	I was in the sea for ten days. Now I have reached an island. But is this a safe place? I don't know.
Calypso:	Hello. My name is Calypso. What has happened to you?
Odysseus:	I have just swum to this island. My name is Odysseus. I am travelling to my home.
Calypso:	Where is your ship?
Odysseus:	There was a terrible storm. My ship disappeared under the water and all the sailors drowned.
Calypso:	That is dreadful. Come to my home. My parents will look after you.
Odysseus:	Thank you. You are very kind. I am exhausted, it's true.

Rewritten from The adventures of Odysseus, a Greek legend adapted by Gill Munton (Macmillan English Explorers, level 4)

Reading comprehension and vocabulary

1 Answer the questions.

1 Which country did Odysseus come from?

2 Why was he away from his wife and son for many years?

3 How was Odysseus travelling home?

4 Who were travelling with him in the ship?

5 Where did the monster with six heads live?

6 What did the six-headed monster sound like?

7 Why did the ship turn over?

8 How long was Odysseus in the sea?

9 What place did he reach?

10 Who helped him?

2 Talk about the answers to these questions.

1 Do you think Odysseus was brave? Why or why not?

2 Why did the ship spin round and round?

3 What do you think was the most frightening:

   a the six-headed monster?   **b** the whirlpool monster?   **c** the storm?
Why?

4 Why do you think Odysseus was the only one who did not drown?

3 Read these words from the play. Match them with the words below.

horrifying   dreadful   exhausted   attack   voyage   creature

> Some words have meanings that are nearly the same as other words.

1 tired   _____

2 journey   _____

3 fight   _____

4 animal   _____

5 terrifying   _____

6 awful   _____

Grammar

1 Look and read.

I love grammar. Do you?

The ship has just passed the cave.
The men have not escaped yet.
They have not seen the monster yet.

They have just seen the monster!

2 Look, read and match. Write the letters.

1 The monster has not grabbed a sailor yet.
2 The monster has just grabbed a sailor.
3 The ship has not disappeared yet.
4 The ship has just disappeared.
5 Odysseus has not reached the island yet.
6 Odysseus has just reached the island.

a  b

c  d

e  f

1 _____ 2 _____ 3 _____

4 _____ 5 _____ 6 _____

3 Ask and answer.

Use your own ideas!

seen

What has he just seen?

He's just seen a monster.

Ow!

1 heard 2 eaten 3 seen 4 found 5 hurt

Grammar in conversation

1 🎧 Listen and read.

Molly: Have you done your Maths homework yet?

Sam: No, not yet. It's really hard. Have you done yours?

Molly: Yes, I've just finished it.

Sam: How about English?
Have you written that composition yet?

Molly: Yes, I've just handed it in. Have you done yours?

Sam: No, not yet.
And I haven't started my Art project yet.

Molly: What about our Science homework?
Have you started that?

Sam: No, not yet. And I haven't revised for the test.

Molly: Test? What test?

Sam: Don't worry! I'm only joking ... Or am I ...?

2 Think, write and say.

What school work do you have to do this week?

I have to write a composition.

We have to revise for a test.

Have you finished your work yet?

I've written my composition.

I've just done my Maths homework

3 Let's talk.

Have you done your Science homework yet?

No, not yet. How about you?

Useful phrases

done   written   started

revised   finished   handed in

What/How about ...?   Don't worry!

Spelling

We can add dis to the beginning of some words. We make a new word with the opposite meaning.

appear ➡ **dis**appear

The ship disappeared under the water.

1 **Add *dis* to these words to make opposites. Read the words.**

_____ like   _____ obey   _____ appear   _____ agree   _____ trust

Listen and say the words.

2 **Write each word in Activity 1 next to the correct definition.**

1 to go from view _____

2 to feel that someone or something is not nice _____

3 to have a different opinion about something _____

4 to feel that someone or something is not good or true _____

5 to not do what someone has asked you to do _____

3 **Choose a word from Activity 2 to complete each sentence.**

1 "That pink dress is awful. I really _____ it."

"I _____. I think it's very pretty."

2 You should never _____ your teacher.

3 In the spring the snow will _____ from the mountains.

4 **Listen and say.**

Have you made your bed yet?
Have you phoned your dad yet?
Have you walked the dog yet?
Have you found my phone yet?
Have you read that book yet?
Have you done the dishes yet?

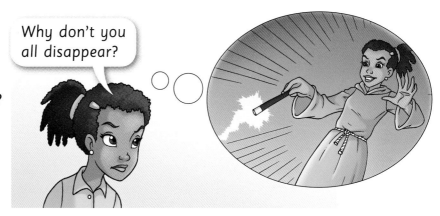

Why don't you all disappear?

Class composition

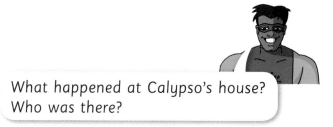

What happened at Calypso's house?
Who was there?

1 **Look at the pictures. Talk about them.**

2 **Write the third scene of the play. Start like this**

Scene: _____

Setting: _____

Characters: _____

Calypso: Mother, Father, this is _____

1 Look and read. 2 🎧 Look, listen and read. 3 Talk about the story.

Uncle Bertie goes to the funfair – Part 2

A legend from the ancient world

Reading

The Trojan Horse

The Greeks fought the Trojans
and year after year,
Troy was surrounded,
its people in fear.

But in darkness one night,
without any warning,
the Greeks packed their ships
and were gone by the morning.

The Trojans walked out
of their city next day
and laughed in amazement,
"The Greeks ran away!"

But something was left.
In silence it stood,
vast and intriguing,
a horse made of wood.

Nobody knew
just why it was there.
Some wondered and worried
but most didn't care.

"It's so magnificent!"
"It's such a size!"
"We are victorious!"
"This is our prize!"

They dragged it through
the tall city gate.
"This horse that we've captured
will never escape!"

The war-weary people
felt only joy.
Till late in the evening
they were dancing in Troy.

Night fell. All slept.
None heard the faint sound.
The wooden horse opened.
Greeks leapt to the ground.

Odysseus, the hero,
led his men out.
They silenced the guards
before they could shout.

Then they opened the gate
and their army rushed past.
The Trojans despaired,
the truth clear at last:

"The Greeks never left!"
"Their horse was a ploy!"
"With their horse they have captured
our city of Troy!"

Who is it?

One Greek hero,
Daring and brave,
Young and strong,
Sailed across the sea.
Saw hideous monsters,
Escaped from a whirlpool,
Unhappy away from home,
Said goodbye to Calyspo and left.

Reading comprehension and vocabulary

1 **Circle the correct answer a or b.**

The Trojan Horse

1	The Greeks surrounded ...	**a** the Trojans	**b** the city of Troy
2	The Greek army was gone ...	**a** by the morning	**b** in the night
3	The Greeks left behind ...	**a** a ship	**b** a horse
4	The horse stood ...	**a** in silence	**b** in a wood
5	The Trojans dragged the horse through ...	**a** the city	**b** the gate
6	Odysseus and his men ...	**a** shouted at the guards	**b** silenced the guards
7	Odysseus and his men opened the gates for ...	**a** the Greek army	**b** the Trojan army
8	The Greek army rushed ...	**a** into Troy	**b** out of Troy

Who is it?

9	Odysseus saw hideous ...	**a** creatures	**b** monsters
10	Odysseus was unhappy away from his ...	**a** home	**b** house

2 **Talk about the answers to these questions.**

1 Where did the Trojans think the Greeks had gone?
2 Where do you think the Greeks went?
3 Who were in the wooden horse?
4 What two things did Odysseus and his men do after they got out of the horse?

3 **Read these words from the poems. Match them with the opposite word below.**

darkness	vast	hideous	silence	drag

1 light _____
2 tiny _____
3 beautiful _____
4 noise _____
5 push _____

Some words have the opposite meaning to other words.

Grammar

1 Look and read.

Hi! Let's look at some grammar!

The Greeks have built a horse. It is made of wood.

The Greeks have built a horse which is made of wood.

The Greeks have built a horse that is made of wood.

This horse will never escape. We've captured it.

This horse that we've captured will never escape.

This horse which we've captured will never escape.

2 Complete the sentences. Write the letters.

1 The sailors saw a monster …   A … that Uncle Bob drives.

2 My aunt has got a parrot …   B … that his grandfather gave him.

3 Meg likes music …   C … that are found in deserts.

4 That is the kind of car …   D … which had six heads.

5 Camels are animals …   E … which she can dance to.

6 John has lost the watch …   F … which can talk.

1 _____ 2 _____ 3 _____ 4 _____ 5 _____ 6 _____

3 Make one sentence.

1 The test was very hard.   … which we had last week …

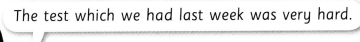

The test which we had last week was very hard.

2 The trainers were expensive.   … which Sam bought …

3 The cakes are always delicious.   … which Grandma makes …

4 The wooden horse was huge.   … that the Greeks built …

5 The monster had six heads.   … that lived in the cave …

6 The snakes are not dangerous.   … that live on this island …

Grammar in conversation

1 🎧 **Listen and read.**

> **Sam:** Have you seen any good films recently?
>
> **Molly:** Yes, I have. I've seen *Journey into space*.
>
> **Sam:** Oh, wow! What's it like?
>
> **Molly:** Oh, it's such a good film! I really enjoyed it.
>
> **Sam:** Do you think I'd like it?
>
> **Molly:** Yes! It's brilliant! The story is wonderful
> and the actors are great.
> And the special effects! They're so incredible!
>
> **Sam:** It sounds amazing.
>
> **Molly:** It is. And there are such scary monsters!
>
> **Sam:** Really? Hmm …Maybe I'll give it a miss …

2 **Think, write and say.**

What films have you seen recently?

> I've seen *Shrek*.

What's it like?

> It's such a good film! It's so funny!

These words can help you:

awful   exciting   boring   good

brilliant

incredible   amazing   terrible   bad

fantastic

3 **Let's talk!**

> Have you seen any films recently?

> Yes, I have. I've seen …

Useful phrases

Oh, wow!

Really?

It sounds …

Maybe

Spelling

> We can add *er* to the end of some verbs.
> The new word is a noun.
> The noun is the person who does the action.

fight + er ➡ fighter

Odysseus was a fighter in the Greek army.

1 **Add *er* to these verbs. Write the nouns.**

 sing ____

_____

 paint ____

_____

 build ____

_____

2 **For some verbs ending in *e*, we just add *r* to make a noun.**

 dance + r ➡ dancer

Make these verbs into nouns. Write the words.

 bake ____

_____

 ride ____

_____

3 **If the verb ends with a short vowel + consonant, double the final consonant. Add *er*.**

 run + n + er ➡ run<u>n</u>er

Make these verbs into nouns. Write the words.

 swim ____

_____

 win ____

_____

🔊 **Listen and say the words.**

4 🔊 **Listen and sing.**

She's a dancer, she's a dancer.
Shadow, shadow, dance with me!
She's a singer, she's a singer,
Shadow, shadow, sing with me!

Run with me, jump with me,
Play with me, stay with me.
Always with me, never leave me,
Shadow, shadow, follow me!
Shadow, shadow, follow me!

Do you remember?
You read an acrostic poem about Odysseus on page 67.

The lines of an acrostic poem do not have to rhyme.
The first letter of the first word in each line is important.
All the first letters spell a word.

1 Read this acrostic poem.

Moving forwards,
Old and angry,
Nose twitching,
Smoke rising.
Terrifying!
Everyone,
Run!

Look carefully at the lines.
Notice the words in the lines.

Lines are not complete sentences.   **Moving forwards,**
Some lines have several words.   **Old and angry,**
Some lines are one word only.   **Terrifying!**

Think of ideas for each letter.
Write them on the board.
Choose the best ideas.

2 Write an acrostic poem about sailors.

S_____
A_____
I_____
L_____
O_____
R_____
S_____

1 Look and read.   2 🎧 Look, listen and read.   3 Talk about the story.

Uncle Bertie goes to the funfair – Part 3

Why did you take the old lady's bag?

She mustn't get Big Sid's doll.

We must find the doll!

Look! Up there on the Big Wheel!

I've got you at last!

We must call the police.

We must stop the Big Wheel.

Why have we stopped?

Help!

Help!

KEEP OUT!

She's up there.

Let's bring her down.

Come with us, please, Madam.

Let me go!

I know you...

Ernie Scruggs!

You should look in her bag.

That was the best birthday ever!

Allow me...

It wasn't me! It was Big Sid!

Revision 3

Digging in the ruins

Ben	Have you found anything yet, Dad?
Dad	Yes, I've just found part of a bowl ...
Meg	Isn't it a whole bowl?
Dad	No. I've never found a complete bowl here.
Meg	Why not?
Dad	Because the people that lived here threw things away into this trench. They only threw away broken things.
Ben	Have you ever found something that wasn't broken?
Dad	No, I haven't yet. If I find a complete bowl here, I will be very lucky.
Meg	It's taking a long time to uncover it.
Ben	You have to do it slowly. If you don't do it slowly, the piece might break again.
Dad	That's right. Look I'm going to lift it out now, very carefully ... Here it is.
Ben	Look Dad, there's something underneath.
Dad	So there is. I'll brush it gently to get the sand off.
Meg	What is it?
Dad	Hmm ... I think it's a little clay horse.
Ben	A horse?
Dad	Yes, look. I think it was a child's toy.
Meg	It's so pretty!
Ben	Have you just discovered a great treasure, Dad?
Dad	It's certainly very rare.
Meg	I wonder why the child left it here.
Ben	Perhaps he threw it away.
Meg	But it isn't broken. What do you think, Dad?
Dad	I don't know. There are questions that you can never answer.
Ben	Archaeology is such an interesting job! I'm going to be an archaeologist, too.

Listening

1 **Look, read and say.**

Sarah Day is a reporter. She is going to
interview Professor Stephen Jones.
He is an archaeologist. What questions
do you think she will ask him?

2  **Listen to the interview and answer the questions.**

1 When did Professor Jones first become interested in archaeology?

2 Does he travel very much to do his work?

3 What can't the professor do?

3 **Listen again and choose the best answer.**

1 Professor Jones found a gold ring
   a in the sea.
   b under a sandcastle.
   c on the beach.

2 The most interesting thing that the professor has ever found was
   a a mask.
   b a statue.
   c a ship.

3 The professor found a huge statue
   a in a desert in Peru.
   b in Egypt.
   c in South America.

4 The Esmeralda is
   a a ship.
   b a treasure.
   c a woman.

5 The professor wants to find the Esmeralda because
   a it is four hundred years old.
   b it was carrying a great treasure.
   c it sank in a terrible storm.

4 **Act out the interview with Professor Jones.**

Now you can do the
project on page 132

Hold the front page!

Two thousand years ago

There were no newspapers. When something important happened, people told each other about it. News travelled slowly. Sometimes it was weeks before people heard about a battle or the death of a king.

More than a thousand years ago

The Chinese government wrote news on silk. It was news about what the government was doing. It did not tell people about other things that were happening.

Four hundred years ago

The first newspaper appeared in Germany. It was printed every week. It took a long time to print all the copies.

Two hundred years ago

The new printing presses could print much more quickly and newspapers were sold on the streets every day.

Now

We have newspapers in the morning and in the evening every day of the week and millions of papers are sold all over the world. Some newspapers have lots of pages and sometimes there is a separate magazine inside it, too.

Reporters go to the scene of a news story and find out what happened. They write about it and photographers take pictures. The editor reads the reporters' work and decides what will be in the paper. If there are mistakes, the editor will change some words. Sometimes an editor says, "Hold the front page!" This means a story is very good and will appear on the front page instead of something else. It is very exciting for the reporter who wrote it.

The story on the next page was written by a young reporter. It is front page news!

Lucky to be alive!

Joe Carver, rescued yesterday from the Blackdown Hills

A father and daughter saved the life of an injured climber yesterday. "Their quick actions prevented a terrible disaster," said Bill Day of the Search and Rescue Team.

Jenny Brown found the phone that saved the climber's life.

Jenny Brown and her father were walking in the Blackdown Hills yesterday. They found rock climber, Joe Carver, lying at the bottom of Blackdown Cliff. Jenny said, "We haven't got a mobile phone, so we couldn't call anyone. The man was unconscious and he had bad injuries."

While her father was putting a blanket over the man, Jenny noticed a mobile phone under his body. When she pulled it from under him, she realised it was connected to the Search and Rescue Team.

Team leader Bill Day said, "Joe Carver phoned us but then he suddenly stopped speaking. We didn't know where he was. We waited for a long time. Then we heard Jenny's voice."

The rescue helicopter went straight to the cliffs and picked up the climber. Pilot Fred Hall said, "I have been in the rescue team for twenty years and Joe Carver is the luckiest man I know. Snow was starting to fall and he almost died of cold."

Last night Joe Carver was recovering in hospital. He said, "I have climbed mountains since 2001. I have never fallen before but I won't climb alone next time."

Blackdown Cliff where Joe Carver fell

The Search and Rescue Team helicopter picked up the injured man

Reading comprehension and vocabulary

1 **Read the sentences. Write *true* or *false*.**

1 Two thousand years ago newspapers travelled slowly. _____

2 The Chinese government wore silk. _____

3 The first newspaper appeared in Germany. _____

4 Four hundred years ago newspapers were printed every day. _____

5 Sometimes there is a separate magazine inside a newspaper. _____

6 The reporter decides what will go in the paper. _____

7 Jenny Brown and her father were walking in the Blackdown Hills last week. _____

8 Jenny used her phone to speak to the Search and Rescue Team. _____

9 The helicopter took the injured man to hospital. _____

10 Joe Carver has fallen several times before. _____

2 **Talk about the answers to these questions.**

1 How many newspapers can you name?

2 Do you ever look at the sports page in a newspaper?

3 Which word do you think describes Jenny best? Why?

   a brave   **b** clever   **c** kind

4 Why do you think Joe Carver said:
   "I won't climb alone next time."

3 **Choose the best word to complete these sentences.**

> mistake   search   magazine   editor   decided   rescue

1 Ben's favourite _____ is all about planes.

2 A helicopter went to _____ the sailors from the sinking ship.

3 Anna _____ to join the basketball club.

4 Mum lost her ring and we had to _____ for it everywhere.

5 The _____ put the news story about the fire on the front page.

6 Always correct a _____ when you notice it.

Grammar

1 Look and read.

It's time for grammar again!

I have been in the rescue team for twenty years.
I have lived in Blackdown for thirty years.

Joe Carver has climbed mountains since 2001.
He has been in hospital since yesterday evening.

2 Answer the questions. Use *for* or *since*.

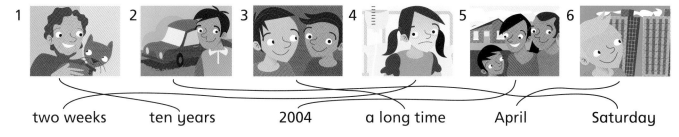

1	2	3	4	5	6
two weeks	ten years	2004	a long time	April	Saturday

1 How long has she had her cat?
2 How long has he had that car?
3 How long have they been friends?
4 How long has she been in hospital?
5 How long have they lived in their house?
6 How long has he lived in New York?

She's had her cat for ten years.

3 Read, ask and answer. Use *for* or *since* in the answer. Use the verbs in brackets.

1 Fred came to Blackdown thirty years ago. (live)

How long has Fred lived in Blackdown?

He's lived in Blackdown for thirty years.

2 Sam started playing the guitar six months ago. (play)
3 Miss Brown came to this school in 2007. (be)
4 Grandpa bought his car twenty years ago. (have)
5 People first arrived on this island hundreds of years ago. (live)
6 The children began to study French in September. (study)

1  **Listen and read.**

Molly:	Have you always lived in Blackdown?
Sam:	No. When I was little, we lived in a village in the country.
Molly:	So how long have you lived here?
Sam:	We've lived here for eight years.
Molly:	Do you live in a house or an apartment?
Sam:	We've got an apartment in Sun Street. It's on the top floor.
Molly:	Lucky you! We're on the ground floor.
Sam:	Where do you live?
Molly:	In that new apartment block in Park Road. We've been there since August.

2 **Think, write and say.**

Where do you live?

I live in Hill Street.

Do you live in a house or an apartment?

I live in a house.

My family lives in an apartment.

Is it big or small?
Has it got a garden?

Which floor do you live on?
Have you got a balcony?

We've lived there for ages.

How long have you lived there?

3 **Let's talk!**

Where do you live?

I live in River Lane.

Useful phrases		
How long…?	since	for
Which floor…?	Lucky you!	

Spelling

Compound nouns are made from two words put together.

news + paper = newspaper

1 Write these compound nouns. Read the words.

snow + man = _____   news + paper = _____

foot + ball = _____   sun + glasses = _____

tooth + ache = _____   super + market = _____

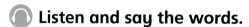

Listen and say the words.

2 Write the words.

1  _____   2 _____   3 _____

4 _____   5 _____   6  _____

3 Listen and say.

I call it an igloo.

Big house, small house.
Very, very tall house.
Castle, cottage,
Hole-in-the-wall house.
Houseboat, boat house,
Snow house, tree house.
Palace, penthouse.
Dog house, greenhouse,
Home!

I call it a nest.

Class composition

Do you remember Jenny Brown? She helped to save a man's life.

1 Read the newspaper report on page 77 again.

2 Read what happened next.

The rescue team wanted to thank Jenny Brown. She was invited to the Search and Rescue Centre. She went with her father and she met the team leader, Bill Day, and the helicopter pilot, Fred Hall. Jenny and her father went up in the rescue helicopter. They flew over Blackdown Cliff.

♣

Blackdown Search and Rescue Team
Certificate of thanks to:

Jenny Brown

for her help in the rescue at Blackdown Cliff

The rescue team showed how they picked up Joe Carver. One of the team went down on a rope. It was very exciting.

They went back to the Centre. Bill Day presented a certificate to Jenny.

3 Write the story for the *Blackdown Daily News*.

1 Write a headline. This tells the reader what the story is about. It is usually only a few words.

2 Write a short first paragraph. This tells the reader a little more about the story. Try to make it interesting so that the reader wants to read the whole report.

3 Write the report of Jenny's visit to the Search and Rescue Centre. Write what happened. Write what these people said about the visit.

Jenny

Bill Day

Fred Hall

4 Think of a photo to put with the report. Write a caption for the photo.

1 Look and read. **2** 🔘 Look, listen and read. **3** Talk about the story.

Tim v Slug – Part 1

You're a bully, Slug! Leave him alone!

Don't worry about him. He's just jealous.

Excellent work, Tim!

Very bad work, Kevin.

Hello, Snail.

On Monday...

Where's my lunch?

On Tuesday...

Where's my sports kit?

On Wednesday...

Where's my English homework?

You must stay after school and do it again.

After school...

It's not fair.

That evening...

I'm fed up with Slug and Snail.

We'll get our revenge.

Reading

News and entertainment

People used to read the news only in the newspapers. When radio was invented, they heard the news. When television was invented, they saw it, too. News programmes are popular, with lots of interviews and reports. Some channels show news and nothing else.

As well as news, there is a lot of entertainment on radio and television. You can hear plays on the radio. The actors are in a studio. They speak into a microphone. You can't see them so you have to imagine the scene for yourself. A sound engineer adds sound effects. They help you to imagine the scene.

Everything is shown to you in a TV drama and you don't need to imagine the scene or what people look like. Sometimes the settings are fascinating places and the costumes are often beautiful. They make the programme very entertaining, especially when there is fast action, too.

People enjoy chat shows in a TV studio. The guests are interviewed by the show's host and their conversations are usually interesting and entertaining. Paddy Riley hosts the chat show, *Paddy's People*. He invites several different people onto his show every week and he always includes a young person. This week he is interviewing an ice skater.

Paddy: My young guest this week is a champion skater who will represent his country at the next Olympics. He's only thirteen years old.

Let me introduce you to Danny Green! (*Audience applauds*) Welcome to the show, Danny.

Danny: Thanks, Paddy.

Paddy: Tell us about your skating, Danny. When did you start?

Danny: When I was four. I went with my sister. We were such noisy children that Mum wanted to get rid of us both on Saturday mornings! (*Audience laughs*)

Paddy: Did you always like it?

Danny: Yes I did, right from the beginning. My sister gave up after a couple of years but I carried on.

Paddy: When was your first competition?

Danny: When I was six.

Paddy: Did you win?

Danny: Yes.

Paddy: So a winner from the start?

Danny: Well ...

Paddy: You're a very modest boy, Danny.

Danny: Oh, ... am I?

Paddy: You've won five gold medals!

Danny: Well, ... that's true ...

Paddy: And that's just in the last three years, ladies and gentlemen! We've got a picture of you, Danny, winning at the international competition last month.

There it is, isn't that fantastic? (*Audience applauds*) How does it feel to be all alone out there with all eyes on you, Danny? Does it make you nervous?

Danny: I'm always nervous before I start, but as soon as I hear the music and start moving, I love it.

Paddy: And we can see why, Danny, you're obviously a born champion. Good luck for the future.

Danny: Thanks very much.

Paddy: Danny Green, ladies and gentlemen, a star to watch. (*Audience applauds*)

Next week I'll talk to a very special young lady. The young lady is a violinist. She's the youngest solo violinist with the City Orchestra. Her name is Meg Thorp. Till then, goodbye and thanks for watching!

Reading comprehension and vocabulary

1 **Match the sentence beginnings and endings.**

1 People used to read the news   a   in a TV drama.

2 Some channels show news   b   on the radio.

3 You can hear plays   c   in a TV studio.

4 The actors are   d   fascinating places.

5 Everything is done for you   e   by the show's host.

6 Sometimes the settings are   f   in a studio.

7 People enjoy chat shows   g   only in the newspapers.

8 The guests are interviewed   h   and nothing else.

1 _____ 2 _____ 3 _____ 4 _____ 5 _____ 6 _____ 7 _____ 8 _____

2 **Think about the answers to these questions.**

1 Which do you like better, radio or television? Why?

2 What kind of programmes do you like?

3 What is your favourite programme?

4 Do you think that Danny is modest? Why or why not?

3 **Complete these sentences about Danny Green.**

Danny's sport is _____. He is a _____ skater. He will represent his country at

the next _____. He started skating when he was _____. He won his first

_____ at the age of _____. He has won five _____ medals in the

last _____ years. He always feels _____ before he starts skating but when he

hears the _____ and starts moving, he _____ it.

Unit 8   Reading comprehension and vocabulary: sentence matching; personal response; cloze

Grammar

1 Look and read.

Guess what! More grammar!

Look! No article!

Paddy Riley has a chat show on TV.
The chat show is called *Paddy's People*.
Today he is interviewing an ice skater.
The ice skater is called Danny Green.
Paddy likes talking to people.
The people on his show are always interesting.

2 Look, ask and answer.

May Owen　　Danny Green　　Ellie Marks　　Jon West　　Rosanna　　Lucky Lee

Is there a singer on the show?

Yes, there is.

What's the singer called?

The singer's called Rosanna.

1 singer　　2 photographer　　3 ice skater　　4 guitarist　　5 painter　　6 actor

3 Talk about *Paddy's People*.

He interviews guests. The guests are interesting.

1　Who does Paddy interview?
2　Where do they sit?
3　What are there on the table?
4　Who performs on the show?
5　Who else performs?
6　What does Danny tell?

1　guests – interesting
2　chairs – comfortable
3　flowers – not real
4　dancers – entertaining
5　musicians – excellent
6　jokes – funny

Grammar in conversation

1 🎧 Listen and read.

Daisy: I've just read a fantastic book.
In fact, it was so fantastic that I read it twice.

Ken: Really? What's the name of this amazing book?

Daisy: Millie Mason – girl reporter.

Ken: Tell me about it.

Daisy: Well, it's about a girl – Millie Mason.
The police can't solve a crime but she can.

Ken: Is it funny?

Daisy: Oh yes! It's such a funny story that I was laughing out loud.

Ken: Who's it by?

Daisy: It's by Henry Jones. He writes such good stories that I only read books by him at the moment.

Ken: Can I borrow it?

Daisy: Of course you can.

2 Think, write and say.

What sort of books do you like?

I like adventure stories.

I like science fiction.

Who is your favourite author?

Roald Dahl.

What's your favourite book?
What's it about?

Matilda. It's about a little girl and how she finds happiness.

3 Let's talk!

What sort of books do you like?

I like books about animals.

Useful phrases

an exciting story

interesting characters

a happy ending

Who's it by?

What's it about?

Unit 8   Grammar in conversation: *so / such a / such … that…*

Spelling

Some words end with the letters el.

chann**el**

Some channels show news and nothing else.

1 Add the letters *el* to complete these words. Write the words. Read the words.

tunn _____   hot _____   trav _____   chann _____   cam _____   lab _____

_____   _____   _____   _____   _____   _____

🎧 **Listen and say the words.**

2 Write the words in Activity 1 next to the correct picture.

1 _____   2 _____   3 _____

4 _____   5 _____   6 _____

3 Write the words in Activity 1 next to the correct definition.

1 a pathway for sending out programmes on TV _____

2 a large tube under the ground that things can travel through _____

3 a short note that is put on something to explain what it is _____

4 a large building with a lot of bedrooms where people can stay _____

5 a large animal that can live in areas where there is little water _____

6 to go on a journey _____

4 🎧 Listen and sing.

His name is Daniel and he's a spaniel.
It's such a perfect name you must agree.
He is a spaniel whose name is Daniel
And Daniel's the spaniel for me.
It's not Buster, Bob or Bill, not Tommy,
    Toots or Ted,

It's not Cracker, Mackaracka, Dominacker,
    Finn or Fred.
It's Daniel, his name is Daniel
And Daniel's the spaniel for me.

Class composition

Paddy Riley is the host of the chat show, *Paddy's People*.

This week his interviewee is Meg Thorp. She is 14 years old. She is a very good violinist. She has just made a CD recording with the City Youth Orchestra.

1 What does Paddy Riley say to introduce Meg Thorp?

Think of one or two sentences.

2 What questions could Paddy ask Meg?

1 Write your ideas in the box.

2 Share your ideas. Choose 4 or 5 of the best questions.

3 What does Meg reply?

Write answers to the questions.

4 Talk about these questions. Discuss and decide.

Does Paddy show the audience a picture of Meg?
Does he play part of the CD recording?
Does Meg play her violin during the interview?
What does the audience do during the interview: applaud? laugh?

5 What does Paddy say at the end of the interview?

Write one or two sentences.

6 Write the interview.

Set it out like a play. Write the names on the left. Write the words they say.
Begin like this: _Paddy: Hello, everyone. My young guest this week is_ _____

1 Look and read.   **2** 🎧 Look, listen and read.   **3** Talk about the story.

Tim v Slug – Part 2

Revision 4

In the news

A burning firework started the fire. The firework landed on the roof.

The firemen have been here for six hours. They went inside the building to make sure that there was no one in it.

Mr Green has owned the factory for ten years.

The firemen are such brave men that they went inside the factory while it was burning.

How long have you lived here, Mrs Day?

We have lived here since 2006. There has never been a fire here before. Harry heard the firework.

The firework was so loud that I woke up.

... and it was such a big fire that the flames were seen from ten kilometres away. This is Fred Jones reporting for City Radio news.

Listening

1 Look, read and say.

Sally Morgan is a TV presenter. She presents a TV programme for children called "What do you know?" Look at the pictures. What is the programme going to be about today?

Marco Polo 1254 –1324

New Year, London, 2009

2 🎧 **Listen and point to the pictures.**

3 🎧 **Listen again and write T (true) or F (false).**

1 The Chinese made the first fireworks. ____

2 The Chinese first discovered gunpowder 1,000 years ago. ____

3 Marco Polo was an explorer. ____

4 Marco Polo brought fireworks to China from Italy. ____

5 The Italians did not like the fireworks. ____

6 Fireworks are bright and noisy. ____

7 A small crowd of people watched the fireworks at New Year in London. ____

8 The fireworks started at twelve o'clock. ____

4 🎧 **Listen again. Number these words in the order you hear them.**

explode   gunpowder   colourful   midnight   fireworks   start   history

____   ____   ____   ____   _|_   ____   ____

5 Talk about it.

Do you like fireworks? Why?/Why not? When and where did you last see fireworks?

> Now you can do the project on page 133

9 Deep sea animals

Reading

Deep Sea Discovery

"It's going to be boring!" complained Jack. "I hate museums."

"It's not a museum, it's an aquarium," Dad explained.

"Same thing," muttered Jack. "It'll be boring anyway."

"There's a new exhibition," said Molly. 'It's called Deep Sea Discovery. It was designed by scientists. You can operate a camera that is deep in the sea. I'd like to go there first."

"Good idea," said Dad.

"Huh!" grunted Jack.

It was dim in the Deep Sea Discovery room. There were some video screens with desks in front and some controls. Molly went to the nearest desk and read the instructions. Then she began to work the controls. The black screen turned dark blue.

"There aren't any animals," said Jack. "Come on. This is boring … oh!"

At that moment an astonishing creature swam across the screen. It was red but the colour glowed warmly. It looked like a Chinese lantern. Suddenly, flashes of colour ran up its tentacles. It was as bright as an electric sign in the street.

"That's so beautiful," whispered Molly.

"Wow!" exclaimed Jack, pointing at the screen "Look at that!" A strange silver animal began to cross the screen. It was long and flat. It had lots of tiny tentacles along both sides of its narrow body. It flapped gently up and down as it moved through the water. It looked like a long silver wave.

"This control turns the camera," said Molly and she turned it away from the silver creature that was already disappearing into the gloom.

"Can I have a go?" asked Jack.

"Of course," replied Molly and she got up to let Jack sit down.

For the next hour they watched one strange creature after another. There were crabs with such small bodies and such long thin legs that they looked like giant spiders. There was an eel with a long thin tail and an enormous head and mouth. Its mouth was so big that it could eat fish as big as itself.

There were tiny squid that made light in their own bodies. They shone like little flashing stars. There was a small furry sponge. There were big squid and jellyfish that you could nearly see right through. Some of them had long hairy tentacles. They floated around picking up bits of food. One jellyfish looked like a plastic bag with eyes. Another one looked like a big round cushion.

There was an incredible creature that looked like a flower. It was called a sea lily but it was an animal. The parts of it that looked like leaves and a flower were actually tiny tentacles. They picked up food and passed it to the animal's mouth in the middle of the flower.

After two hours, Dad said, "Do you want to go soon?"

Jack looked round in surprise. "You're not bored already, are you, Dad?" he asked.

Reading comprehension and vocabulary

1 Who said it? Tick the correct box.   Molly   Dad   Jack

1 It's not a museum, it's an aquarium.

2 It was designed by scientists.

3 Good idea.

4 There aren't any animals

5 That's so beautiful.

6 Look at that!

7 This control turns the camera.

8 Can I have a go?

9 Do you want to go now?

10 You're not bored already, are you?

2 Think about the answers to these questions.

1 Who do you think is older, Jack or Molly? Why?

2 Which do you think is more interesting, an aquarium or a museum? Why?

3 Did Jack change his mind about the aquarium? How do you know?

3 Label the animals and objects from the story.

cushion   squid   tentacle   lantern   sea lily   jellyfish   star   eel

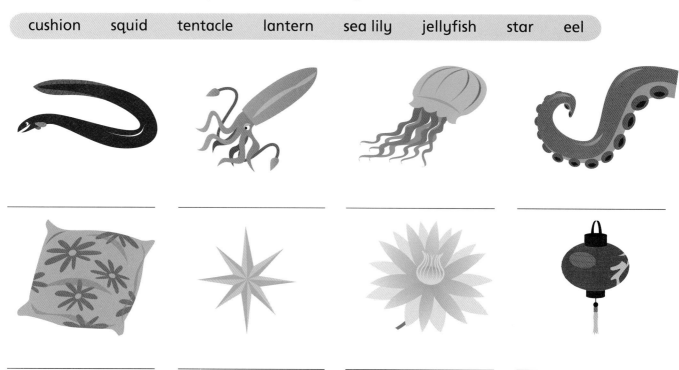

_____   _____   _____   _____

_____   _____   _____   _____

Grammar

1 Look and read.

Yippee! It's grammar time again!

Jack and Molly were taken to the aquarium by their father.
The exhibition was called Deep Sea Discovery.
The exhibition was designed by scientists.

2 Finish the sentences. Write the letters.

1 The aquarium was visited …
2 The sea creatures were filmed …
3 The cameras were placed …
4 The controls were worked …
5 The sea creatures were shown …
6 Molly was fascinated …

A … by the wonderful sea creatures.
B … by visitors in the aquarium.
C … with special cameras.
D … by lots of children.
E … on video screens.
F … deep in the sea.

1 _____ 2 _____ 3 _____ 4 _____ 5 _____ 6 _____

3 Ask and answer.

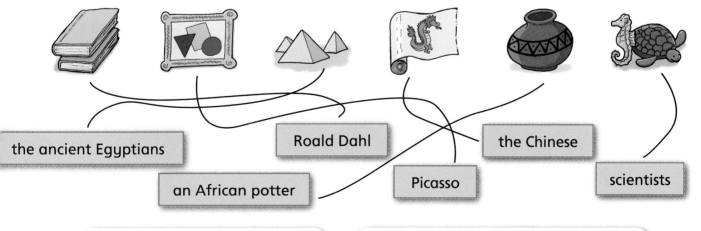

the ancient Egyptians

Roald Dahl

the Chinese

an African potter

Picasso

scientists

Who were the books written by?

The books were written by Roald Dahl.

1 the books – written?   2 the pyramids – built?   3 the sea creatures – filmed?
4 silk – invented?   5 the picture – painted?   6 the pot – made?

Grammar in conversation

1  **Listen and read.**

> **Molly:** What are you going to do at the weekend?
>
> **Sam:** Well, I want to watch a football match.
>
> **Molly:** On TV or at the stadium?
>
> **Sam:** At the stadium. The trouble is I don't think I can.
>
> **Molly:** Why not?
>
> **Sam:** Because I ought to go to my grandma's birthday party.
>
> **Molly:** You can't miss that.
>
> **Sam:** No. How about you? What are you going to do?
>
> **Molly:** Well, I want to go shopping but I'm not sure if I will.
>
> **Sam:** Why not?
>
> **Molly:** Because I need to tidy my bedroom. It's in a terrible mess. And anyway I haven't got any money.
>
> **Sam:** Well, that's that then!

2 Think, write and say.

What are you going to do at the weekend?

I want to go swimming.

I ought to finish my Science project.

I need to revise. We've got a test on Monday.

3 Let's talk!

What are you going to do at the weekend?

Well, ...

Useful phrases

Well ...

The trouble is ...

I'm not sure.

Anyway ...

Some words end with the letters *le*.

tentacle
Some jellyfish have very long tentacles.

1 **Add the letters *le* to complete these words. Write the words.**

tab ____   batt ____   cab ____   bubb ____   stab ____   app ____

_____   _____   _____   _____   _____   _____

Listen and say the words.

2 **Write the words. Read the words.**

3 **Listen and say.**

Billy-Jo and Joby-Lee –
Naughty twins, the age of three.
Visitors say, "Aren't they sweet?"
I say, "Yes, when they're asleep!"
But when they run and scream and shout
And fight and throw their food about
And break their toys and tease the cat
And make a boat with Grandpa's hat
And jump in the mud and splash in a puddle,
They're not sweet. They're double trouble!

Class composition

Molly and Jack were amazed by the creatures they saw in the Deep Sea Discovery exhibition.

1 **Look at the picture. Molly and Jack saw this creature, too.**

2 **Talk about the picture:**

| What colours is it? | | What shape is it? |

| What does it look like? | How do you think it moves? |

Write your ideas on the board.

3 **Think of adjectives to describe the creature. Write them on the board.**

4 **Continue the story.**

• Jack and Molly wanted to stay in the Deep Sea Discovery exhibition a bit longer.

Begin like this:

"Alright," said Dad. "We can stay a bit longer."

Then another fantastic creature swam across the screen. It was ...

• Finish the paragraph describing the creature. Use interesting adjectives in your description.

• What did Molly and Jack say about it? Write their words as direct speech.

1 Look and read.   2 🎧 Look, listen and read.   3 Talk about the story.

Tim v. Slug – Part 3

Reading

The land under the oceans

Light from the sun helps plants to grow underwater. Sunlight can go down through water to about 100 metres. In the water near beaches there are many plants and animals. Below 150 metres there are no plants, only animals. At 300 metres it is already quite dark and the water is very cold.

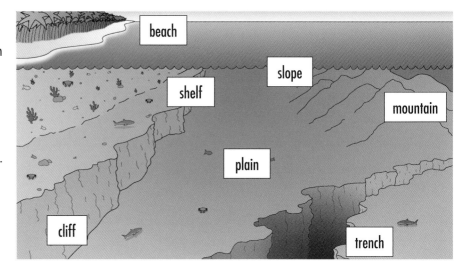

beach

slope

shelf

mountain

plain

cliff

trench

The world's oceans are about 3,000 metres deep.

Out in the oceans there are mountains under the water just like there are mountains on land. In some parts of the ocean there are deep trenches. The deepest trench goes down 11,000 metres. Much of the ocean floor is a plain. It continues for thousands of kilometres but there are few animals there. It is difficult to explore the deep ocean. Water is heavy. If a diver was in water 900 metres deep, the weight of the water above him would crush his body.

One way to explore the deep ocean is to go down in a submersible. Deeper than 1,000 metres there is no sunlight at all. The submersible has lights so the people inside can see what is outside. We can look at pictures of the animals that live in the deep ocean because they are lit up by the machine. If the lights were not on, there would be complete darkness.

This submersible can go down to 4,000 metres.

A chimney can grow by 6 metres in a year.

With a submersible, scientists can look at chimneys. Very hot water escapes into the ocean from below the ocean floor. It is so hot that it looks like smoke from a fire. It has tiny bits of rock in it. Gradually, the tiny pieces build a tall chimney. Many animals like living near these chimneys. There are crabs, octopuses and shellfish but one of the strangest is the tube worm.

Tube worms can grow to 2.4 metres tall.

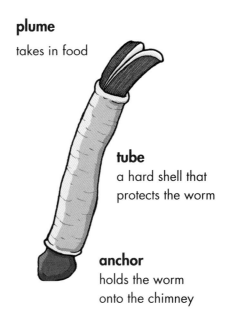

plume
takes in food

tube
a hard shell that
protects the worm

anchor
holds the worm
onto the chimney

A tube worm has no mouth or stomach. It takes food from the water through the top of its body. The top of a tube worm looks like a red feather. It is called a plume, which is another word for a feather.
The worm is protected by its tube which is a hard shell. The bottom of the worm is an anchor that holds the worm onto the chimney.

It takes a long time to go down to 4,000 metres in a submersible and the journey is not comfortable. Scientists are looking for other ways of exploring the ocean floor. Robot machines can go deeper. They do not carry people but they can record a lot of information about the ocean and they can take pictures. One day it may be possible to explore the oceans on a computer screen.

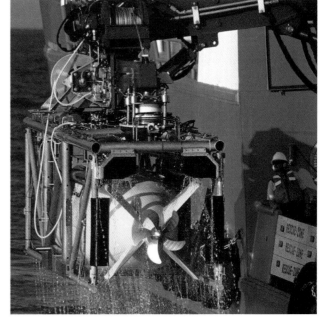

Robot machines are operated from a ship.

Reading comprehension and vocabulary

1 Underline the correct answer.

1	Sunlight can go down through water	a 10 metres	b 100 metres	c 1,000 metres
2	The deepest trench goes down	a 110 metres	b 1,100 metres	c 11,000 metres
3	There is no sunlight at all deeper than	a 1,000 metres	b 150 metres	c 300 metres
4	Animals at 3,000 metres live	a in darkness	b in trenches	c on the ocean floor
5	In a year, a chimney can grow by	a 0.6 metres	b 6 metres	c 16 metres
6	The top of a tube worm looks like a red	a feather	b flower	c firework
7	Robot machines can be operated from	a a computer	b a ship	c a submersible
8	Scientists are looking for other ways of exploring	a chimneys	b the oceans	c the ocean floor

2 Think about the answers to these questions.

1 Would you like to travel down to the ocean floor? Why or why not?
2 Do you think tube worms are fascinating, ugly, beautiful or horrible? Why?
3 What information in "The land under the oceans" did you know? What didn't you know?

3 Choose the correct word to complete each sentence.

> bottom   light up   comfortable   pile up   submersible

1 The scientist went down to 2,000 metres in a _____.

2 When fireworks explode they _____ the sky.

2 The teacher said, "Please _____ your books on my desk."

4 This chair is very _____.

5 There was a river at the _____ of the hill.

Grammar

Isn't grammar marvellous?

1 Look and read.

These plants have light. They are growing.
If they did not have light, they would not grow.

In deep oceans, there is not any light.
If you dived very deep, you would not find plants.
Animals can live without light.
If you went down very deep, you would find animals.

2 Find the endings. Write the letters.

1 This plant has not got any water.
If the plant had water, … ☐

2 Ned has not got any money.
If Ned had some money, … ☐

3 It is not sunny.
If it was sunny, … ☐

4 He is not wearing a jacket.
If he was wearing a jacket, … ☐

5 She is not tired.
If she was tired, … ☐

A … we would go to the beach.

B … she would sleep.

C … it would grow.

D … he would not be cold.

E … he would buy a computer game.

3 Finish these sentences. Talk with your friends.

1 If I had a lot of money, I would …

2 If I could go on holiday, I would …

3 If I was twenty-one years old, I would …

Grammar in conversation

1  **Listen and read.**

> **Daisy:** Excuse me, I'm doing a survey.
> Would you mind answering a few questions?
> **Ken:** Not at all.
> **Daisy:** OK. My first question is:
> What do you enjoy doing?
> **Ken:** Let me think ...I enjoy sleeping.
> **Daisy:** Thank you. And what do you hate doing?
> **Ken:** That's easy. I hate getting up early.
> **Daisy:** Hmm ... What do you avoid doing?
> **Ken:** That's tricky ... I avoid running.
> **Daisy:** What? Well, here's my last question.
> What are you looking forward to doing?
> **Ken:** I'm looking forward to lying on the sofa
> and watching TV.
> **Daisy:** Honestly! You're so lazy!
> **Ken:** I love teasing you!

2 Think, write and say.

| What do you enjoy doing? | What do you hate doing? | What do you avoid doing? | What are you looking forward to doing? |

I enjoy swimming.

I hate playing football.

I avoid washing the dishes.

I'm looking forward to going on holiday.

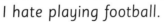

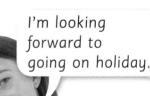

3 Let's talk!

I'm doing a survey. Will you answer my questions?

Sure.

> **Useful phrases**
>
> Would you mind ...?   Not at all.
>
> Let me think ...   That's easy.
>
> That's tricky.   Honestly!

Spelling

> Some words end with the letters *ey* sounding *ee*.

chimney
This is a deep sea chimney.

1 **Complete the words with *ey*. Write the words under the correct picture.**

journ____   chimn____   vall____   k____   donk____

_____ _____ _____ _____ _____

> Only a few words end with the letters *ire*.

fire
The hot water looks like smoke from a fire.

🎧 **Listen and say the words.**

2 **Read these words. Check you understand them.**

fire   wire    umpire

3 🎧 **Listen and sing.**

Lazy Daisy, sleeping by the road,
Doesn't want to carry that heavy load,
No sir, no mam, doesn't want to go
Down to the marketplace.

Lazy Daisy, sleeping in the sun,
Doesn't want to walk, doesn't want to run,
No sir, sir mam, doesn't want to go
Down to the marketplace.

Many animals live on the chimneys deep in the ocean. Scientists have seen this octopus near chimneys.

1 Look at this picture. Talk about it.

• What colour is it? What shape is it? How big are its eyes?

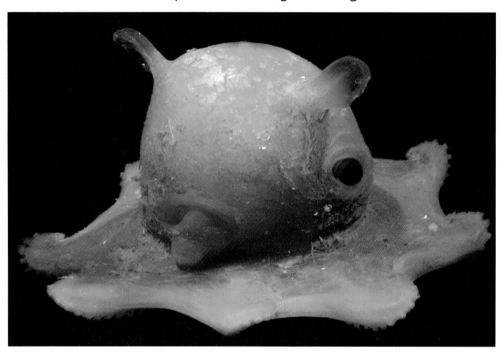

2 Read the notes.

> has two large fins – fins look like big ears
>
> is known as the dumbo octopus – Dumbo the elephant in a Disney film
>
> fins help it to swim – moves slowly
>
> lives in deep sea 100–5,000 m – can grow to 20 cms
>
> eats shellfish, snails, worms – finds these on chimneys
>
> has a strong bite – small, but scientists watched it attack their submersible

3 Write a paragraph about the octopus.

Remember that notes are often phrases. You need to add other words to make complete sentences.

4 Draw a diagram. Label it. Use these words.

    body   fin   eye   tentacle

Write a caption for the diagram.

1 Look and read.   **2** 🎧 Look, listen and read.   **3** Talk about the story.

Diamond Quest – Part 1

The Kingdom of Zarula

King Olaf and Princess Karina

Prince Torgan

Is the king dying?

You will be a very good queen.

You are not alone, Karina.

Silas! Banto! Dear Lilia!

Bring me the Great Diamond of Zarula!

Without the Great Diamond I cannot be Queen.

Someone has stolen the Great Diamond of Zarula!

Soon I will be King!

Revision 5

1 🎧 **Listen and read.** **2 Talk about the story.** **3 Act it.**

I like my work because I like diving in the submersible and I like finding out about things. This octopus was found by a diver at 100 metres. Two new crabs were seen by the same diver.

sea life scientist

I control this submersible. I enjoy working with machines and I love travelling to oceans all over the world. This submersible can go down to 4,000 metres. My job is fantastic!

underwater pilot

Press the button to hear the people talking about their work

Ben	What's this all about?
Sue	You press this button, then you hear these people.
Ben	Have you listened to them?
Sue	Yes. They talked about their work.
Ben	Was it interesting?
Sue	Yes. Well, I thought so, anyway.
Ben	Does the scientist go diving?
Sue	Yes, she does but the submersible is controlled by the pilot.
Ben	If I worked in the ocean I would be a pilot. Does he go down deep?
Sue	Yes, down to 4,000 metres.

Ben	Amazing!
Sue	And he loves travelling to oceans all over the world.
Ben	It sounds a fantastic job!
Sue	If you listened to the recording, Ben, you would hear it all yourself.
Ben	That's OK, you've just told me.
Sue	You are so lazy, Ben! If you were a pilot you would go to the bottom and never come back up.
Ben	That's so unfair! I would come back up and then stay in bed for a day.
Sue	Really, Ben! You are terrible!

Listening

1 Talk about these people. Write the names of their jobs.

| scientist | costume designer | footballer |
| animal trainer | musician | sports photographer |

_____

_____

_____

_____

2 Listen and write the people's names under their jobs.

Pam   Bob   Joe   Sue   Ed   Ann   Nina

3 Listen again and answer the questions.

1 Who won a prize? _____

2 What animal did Ann train recently? _____

3 What does Bob usually do? _____

4 Why isn't he working now? _____

5 What sports doe Joe play? _____

6 What is Pam studying? _____

7 What does she say about them? _____

8 What would Ed like to do? _____

4 Talk about it.

Would you like to do any of these jobs? Why?

Which of these jobs would you not like to do? Why?

Now you can do the project on page 134

11 Helping other people

Mary Seacole

Her early life

Mary Seacole was born in Jamaica in 1805. Her father was a soldier in the British army. Her mother owned a hotel. Many soldiers from the British army stayed there. They were often ill with diseases that are found in hot countries. Mary's mother looked after the soldiers and she made medicines for them. When she was a young girl, Mary watched her mother and learned from her. When she was older she helped her mother to look after the people in the hotel. Sometimes she helped in the British army hospital, too.

Working as a nurse

Mary married Edwin Seacole in 1836. Over the next few years she had many difficulties. The hotel burned down in 1843 and had to be rebuilt. Her husband died in 1844 and her mother died very soon afterwards. Mary was very sad but she decided to work hard. The hotel was now hers. She continued to nurse sick people and she became well-known. She travelled to Central America and nursed many patients there, too. More and more people knew about her work.

A war far away

In 1854 Mary heard about a war far away in the south of Russia. British soldiers were fighting Russian soldiers. Many men were dying in battle. They were dying in the hospitals because of germs and diseases. Mary wanted to help. The doctors in Jamaica said that Mary Seacole was a good nurse. They wrote a letter to the British Government. Mary took it to London but the government would not send her to the war. Mary thought that they did not like her brown skin. She thought they wanted only English nurses.

Helping wounded soldiers

Mary travelled to the war on her own. She visited the hospital of Florence Nightingale, another famous nurse. Florence Nightingale did not want Mary, either. Mary travelled closer to the war. She built her own hotel near to the British Army's camp. She looked after sick and wounded soldiers. She worked hard until the end of the war in 1856.

The return to London

Mary returned to London but she had no money. Many important people knew about her work in the war. There were stories about her in the newspapers. People gave her money. She wrote her autobiography and she recounted all her travels and adventures. She died in 1881.

A heroine at last

People forgot about her for nearly a hundred years. Everyone knew about Florence Nightingale but Mary Seacole's work was not remembered. Recently, that has changed. Now children learn about her in school. New buildings in universities are named after her. When she faced difficulties in her life, she tried harder. She travelled across the world to help other people. She had little money and she was not important but she still helped. Now people think of her as a real heroine.

MAULL & C?   187ᴬ PICCADILLY
AND
62 CHEAPSIDE

Reading comprehension and vocabulary

1 Answer the questions.

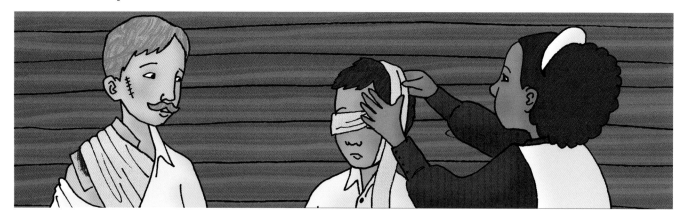

1 Where was Mary Seacole born?

2 What happened in 1843?

3 When did her husband die?

4 Where did she travel to after 1844 and nurse patients?

5 What did the doctors in Jamaica say about Mary Seacole?

6 Which hospital did Mary Seacole visit?

7 What did she write about in her autobiography?

8 How do people think of Mary Seacole now?

2 Think about the answers to these questions.

1 Do you think Mary Seacole was brave? Why or why not?

2 Why do you think people forgot about Mary Seacole after she died?

3 Do you agree that Mary Seacole was a real heroine? Why or why not?

3 Write the words in the correct lists.

disease   soldier   sick   germ   war   ill   fight   battle   patient   camp

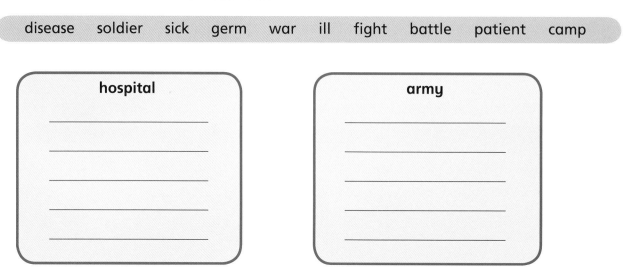

hospital

_____

_____

_____

_____

army

_____

_____

_____

_____

Unit 11   Reading comprehension and vocabulary: literals; personal response; categorising

Grammar

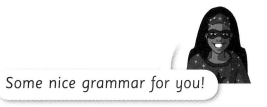

1 Look and read.

Some nice grammar for you!

Mary Seacole is a good nurse.

There is a war in Russia.

The British army hospitals are dirty.

The soldiers are ill.

The doctor said that Mary Seacole was a good nurse.

He said that there was a war in Russia.

Mary said that the British army hospitals were dirty.

She said that the soldiers were ill.

2 Match the speech bubbles and the sentences. Write the letters.

The nurses are kind.

She is from Jamaica.

The doctors are very busy.

The hospital is dirty.

Mary is a good woman.

There are sick soldiers in the hospital.

A   **B**   **C**   **D**   **E**   **F**

1 The doctor said that she was from Jamaica. _____

2 He said that Mary was a good woman. _____

3 Mary said that the hospital was dirty. _____

4 She said that there were sick soldiers in the hospital. _____

5 She said that the nurses were kind. _____

6 She said that the doctors were busy. _____

3 What did Mary say?

She said that…

The war is terrible.

The nurses are tired.

The diseases are awful.

The hospital is old.

The soldiers are brave.

Grammar in conversation

1  **Listen and read.**

Sam:	I met an alien last night.
Molly:	Don't be silly!
Sam:	It's true! He said that he lived under my bed.
Molly:	Don't be ridiculous!
Sam:	He said that he was hungry.
	He said that he wanted a sandwich.
Molly:	Really? And what did you say?
Sam:	I said that I couldn't make him a sandwich.
Molly:	Why not?
Sam:	I said that I had to go to China.
Molly:	What? You're crazy!
Sam:	No, I'm not. But it was a crazy dream!

2 Think, write and say.

Think about a strange dream which you had.
Where were you? Who did you meet?
What did he or she say? What did you say?
What happened next?

I was in the park.

I met an alien.

He said he wanted to play football.

I said I didn't like football.

He disappeared.

3 Let's talk!

Guess what! I had a very strange dream last night.

Really? What happened?

Useful phrases

Guess what!   Really?

Wow!   That's crazy!

Spelling

The letter g sometimes sounds soft. It sounds like j in jump.

g**erm**

Soldiers were dying because of germs and disease.

1 **The soft g sound can be made by:**

g followed by e germ   g followed by i giant   g followed by y gymnast

2 **Soft g can be inside a word. Read these words.**

message   large   vegetable

Write words with hard g in box 1. Write words with soft g in box 2.

engine   gull   game   giraffe   orange   guest   huge   gone

1	2
_____ _____	_____ _____
_____ _____	_____ _____

Listen and check your answers.

3 Listen and say.

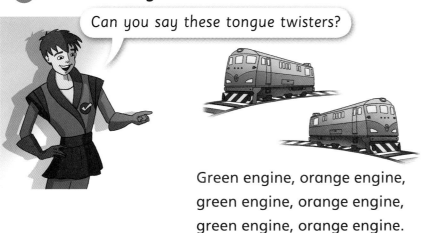

Can you say these tongue twisters?

Green engine, orange engine, green engine, orange engine, green engine, orange engine.

George the giant juggles huge jellybeans.

Class composition

> When Mary Seacole went to help in the war she had to build a hotel herself.

1 **Read the notes about Mary Seacole during the war. Look at the pictures.**

found place for hotel near British Army camp – called it Spring Hill

workmen helped build it – found materials

used: pieces of wood, wooden boxes, metal sheets, old doors, windows from village

hotel had one big room for eating, kitchen, two buildings for sleeping, stable yard

name – the British Hotel – at hotel Mary sold meals, coffee, useful objects

looked after sick people, wounded soldiers

visited wounded soldiers at army camp – men called her 'Mother Seacole'

took food to army camp

helped wounded soldiers at the place of the battle – British and Russian soldiers

2 **Write two paragraphs about Mary Seacole during the war. Begin like this:**

<u>Mary Seacole found a place for her hotel near the British Army camp.</u>

1 Look and read. **2** 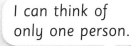 Look, listen and read. **3** Talk about the story.

Diamond Quest – Part 2

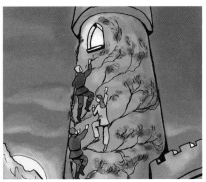

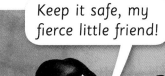

12 Saving other people

The great race of mercy

This is the true story of how twenty mushers and one hundred and fifty dogs saved the lives of 10,000 people in the winter of 1925.

Nome is a small town in the north of Alaska. In January 1925 some children in the town became ill and died. The doctor realised it was a terrible disease. It could quickly infect and kill everybody in the town. Immediately, he sent for medicine. A plane was ready to fly the medicine more than 1,000 km to Nome but the weather was too cold and it could not take off. Only a dog-sledge could take the medicine but everyone asked, "Can the dogs reach Nome in time?"

Twenty teams of husky dogs and mushers ran as a relay. The first team left Nenana on 27 January in a gale and a snowstorm. The dogs raced through the night in -52 C. The next day a new team carried on. The relay continued for four days and nights through thick snow and ice. The newspapers and radio carried the story. They called it The Great Race of Mercy. Everyone wanted the dogs to succeed.

On 31 January the medicine arrived at the coast. The quickest route to Nome was across the bay. It was a vast expanse of frozen sea more than 50 km across. Henry Ivanoff set off with his team but almost at once they ran into a reindeer and got tangled up. Just then Leonard Seppala arrived from the north. He was the most famous and fastest musher. "I have the medicine!" Ivanoff shouted. Seppala took the medicine and turned back towards the north into a raging blizzard.

His lead dog was twelve-year-old Togo. Crossing the frozen sea was the most difficult and dangerous part of the journey. The ice was breaking up. Once, the whole team was stranded on an ice floe. Togo had to jump 1.5 m across freezing water. The harness broke but Togo jumped into the water, took the harness

in his mouth and pulled the ice together until it was safe for the rest of the team to jump. They reached the next team on 1st February. The medicine was quickly carried to the last team which was led by Balto.

Balto was not usually a lead dog and he was only three years old. The musher was not sure that Balto had the strength and obedience of a lead dog. Balto led his team bravely all night and they arrived in Nome early next morning. The medicine was safely delivered. The doctor treated his patients and no more people died.

Afterwards Balto was a hero for a few months. Later he was sold and shown around America but he was badly looked after. Eventually he was rescued and lived in a zoo. All the dogs who ran were heroes. Six of them froze to death on the journey. Togo lived to the age of sixteen. All the husky dogs in America today are descendants of Togo and the other brave runners of 1925.

Reading comprehension and vocabulary

1 Match the sentence beginnings and endings.

1	Nome is a small town	on an ice floe.
2	The doctor realised	it was a terrible disease.
3	Everyone hoped	and no more people died.
4	The quickest route to Nome was	from the north.
5	Just then Leonard Seppala arrived	twelve-year-old Togo.
6	His lead dog was	across the bay.
7	Once the whole team was stranded	in the north of Alaska.
8	The doctor treated his patients	the dogs would succeed.

2 Talk about the answers to these questions.

1 Would you like to ride in a dog-sledge? Why or why not?

2 Which place do you think is more dangerous, the Arctic or the desert? Why?

3 What other animals help people? What do they do?

3 Match the words from the story on the left with their opposite meanings.

1	difficult	_easy_	a live
2	dangerous	_____	b tiny
3	immediately	_____	c wonderful
4	vast	_____	d easy
5	die	_____	e fail
6	terrible	_____	f thin
7	thick	_____	g later
8	succeed	_____	h safe

A word with the opposite meaning to another word is an antonym.

Unit 12 Reading comprehension and vocabulary: sentence matching; personal response; definition

Grammar

1 Look and read.

Hooray! Some more grammar!

More than one hundred dogs took part in the Great Race.
Fewer than ten dogs died.

There was more snow than usual that winter,
but there was less ice on the bay.

2 Ask and answer.

A  B

Which team has more dogs?

Team A has more dogs.

1 more luggage?   2 fewer passengers?   3 less strength?
4 fewer dogs?   5 less luggage?   6 more passengers?

3 Ask and answer.

A  B  C

Which picture has the most snow?

Picture B has the most snow.

1 the most sunshine?   2 the most trees?   3 the least snow?
4 the fewest trees?   5 the least sunshine?   6 the fewest houses?

Grammar in conversation

1 Look at the useful phrases. How many can you use? Work with a friend.

> **Useful phrases**
>
> Well, …   Really?   Wow!   That sounds nice / brilliant / fantastic.   Lucky you!
>
> How about you?   What about you?   Poor you!   Oh dear …   Don't worry!
>
> Never mind!   Nonsense!   … I'm afraid.   Maybe   The trouble is …   Anyway

2  Listen and read.

Ken:	What are you going to do in the holidays?
Daisy:	Well, I'm going to the seaside.
	My aunt has a house right on the beach.
Ken:	Wow! That sounds fantastic. Lucky you!
Daisy:	How about you? What are you going to do?
Ken:	Nothing. I'm going to stay at home.
Daisy:	Oh dear.
Ken:	The trouble is my dad's very busy
	and he can't get away.
Daisy:	Well, never mind.
Ken:	It's going to be so boring.
Daisy:	Nonsense! You'll have a good time.
Ken:	Maybe …
Daisy:	Anyway, I must go. Mum's waiting for me.
Ken:	OK. Bye!

3 Think about it!

What are you going to do in the holidays? Make notes.

4 Let's talk!

What are you going
to do in the holidays?

Well, …

Spelling

Some words begin with silent letters.
We cannot hear the silent letters when we say the words.

knew
The doctor knew he needed more medicine.
We cannot hear the k in knew.

1 Read these words. Check the meanings.

knife	knee
know	kneel

Listen and say the words.

wrapped
The musher wrapped blankets round his dogs.
We cannot hear the w in wrapped.

2 Read these words. Check the meanings.

wreck	wrap
write	wrong

Listen and say the words.

Some words end with a silent b.

clim**b**
In the great race, the dogs had to climb hills.
We cannot hear the b at the end of climb.

3 Read these words. Check the meanings.

lamb	climb
comb	thumb

Listen and say the words.

4 Listen and sing.

The sun is shining.
The sky is blue.
Are we nearly there yet?
I love driving in the car with you
But are we nearly there yet, please?

Where's the sand?
Where's the sea?
Are we nearly there yet?
A golden beach is waiting for me.
Are we nearly there yet, please?

Class composition

Look at what happened when Balto was leading the team.
The driver of Balto's team was Gunaar Kaarson.

1 Talk about the pictures. Make sentences.
Use the notes to help you. Use your own ideas, too.

1 dogs running fast
   – snowing so hard that Kaarson …

2 Balto – led – brave
   – strong – blizzard

3 suddenly the gale blew ….

4 sledge – turned over – medicine fell

5 Kaarson – turned right way up
   – dogs waited

6 horrified – medicine gone

I must find the medicine!

7 searched – bare hands

8 found

9 Balto led again
   – last part of journey to …

2 Write this part of the story.

- Write clear information.
- Describe the setting of the events.
- Explain what happened in simple statements.

Remember!
Use a little direct
speech in your story.

1 Look and read.   **2** 🎧 Look, listen and read.   **3** Talk about the story.

Diamond Quest – Part 3

1 🎧 **Listen and read.**   **2 Talk about the story.**   **3 Act it.**

When Florence was young, she learned Maths. Her teacher said that Florence was a clever girl.

When she was older, she saw many poor people. She told her parents that the poor people needed help.

Florence met an important man. She told him that more people were ill because their homes were dirty.

Florence wanted to be a nurse. She told her father that nurses helped doctors and they saved people's lives.

Florence's father told her that ladies had to marry and stay at home. Later he let Florence become a nurse.

Her hospitals were always clean. She told her nurses that fewer people died when everything was washed well.

Listening

1 Look, read and say.

Mecca   Morocco

twenty-eight years

the Sahara desert

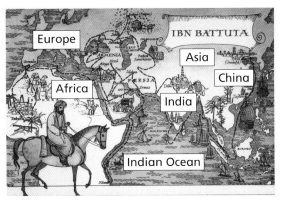

Sultan

Iran   Turkey

Ibn Juzayy

What does this information tell you about Ibn Batuta? Can you guess?

Talk about it like this:

> I think *he was born in Morocco.*

> Perhaps *Ibn Juzayy was a friend of his.*

2 🎧 Listen and answer these questions.

1 Was Ibn Batuta a traveller or a writer?

2 Look at these scenes from his life. What can you say about them?

3 🎧 Listen again and write T (true) or F (false).

1 Ibn Batuta was born in Morocco. _____

2 He was not a good student. _____

3 After his visit to Mecca he went home. _____

4 After he had been to Russia, he travelled to India. _____

5 He stayed in China for a short time. _____

6 His first journey lasted twenty-eight years. _____

7 He did not travel in Africa. _____

8 Ibn Juzayy wrote down his stories. _____

9 During his life he travelled more than 120,000 kilometres. _____

10 He died at the age of 68. _____

4 Talk about it.

Work in pairs. One of you is Ibn Batuta.
The other is Ibn Juzayy. Talk about Ibn Batuta's travels.

Now you can do the project on page 135

Project 1: What happened next?

1 **Read. Choose words to complete the sentences.**

> a professor   an archaeologist   firemen   thieves   exciting   fantastic
>
> a book   a map   a picture   is valuable   shows a place where there is treasure

The next day, the children looked in the newspaper. This is what they read.

Yesterday actors were rehearsing for the new Andy Hall adventure film.

　　Andy Hall is _____ who works in the city museum.

In the new film, two _____ go to the museum to steal _____. They want it because it _____

Andy Hall takes it onto the roof of the museum. He jumps onto the next building and the _____ cannot catch him.

In the rehearsal yesterday, two _____ were helping. Andy Hall jumped across the gap and they caught him. Andy Hall has lots more adventures in this _____ new film.

"Wow!" said Ben. "This new film will be _____!"

"Yes," said Sue. "What do you think happened next?"

"That's easy," said Ben. "This is what happened. Andy Hall escaped from the thieves but the thieves followed him. Andy Hall went …"

2 **Complete Ben's idea for the Andy Hall adventure.**

Read the questions. Write one paragraph about what happened next.

Where did Andy Hall go? Why?

Did the thieves catch Andy Hall? What happened?

Did Andy Hall escape again? How?

3 **Think of a title for the new film. Design a poster for the new film.**

Remember to include the name of most important actor and a picture of something that happens in the film.

Project 2: Bridges and tunnels

1 **Find out about a bridge or a tunnel near you.**

The bridge can be

a small bridge

a big bridge

an old bridge

a new bridge

The tunnel can be

short or long   for cars

for trains

2 **Write facts about the bridge or tunnel.**

How long is it?   How old is it?   What does it cross or go under?

3 **Describe it.**

What is it made of?   What does it look like?   Is there anything special about it?

4 **Write what you think about it.**

Is it beautiful?   ugly?   noisy?   crowded?   interesting?   Why?
Have you used it?   by car?   by train?   by bus?   walking?   What was it like?

5 **Find a picture or draw one.**

6 **Show your work and talk about it.**

This is the ... tunnel.
It goes under the ....
It is ...

This is the ... Bridge.
It crosses the River ....
It is ...

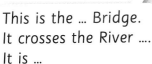

Project 3: People from long ago

1 **Find out about people that lived a long time ago.**

Choose

the ancient Egyptians   the ancient Greeks   or your own idea

2 **Write information about the people.**

Use this list to give you ideas or find out more facts of your own.

Buildings
What did they look like?
How did they build them?

Clothes
What did the men wear?
What did the women wear?

Travel
Did they have boats?
Did they have carts?
What were they like?

Children
Did they go to school?
What did they learn?
What toys did they have?

3 **Draw pictures or find pictures.**

4 **Make a book. Make a cover.**

Project 4: This is what happened

Choose one of these tasks. Use all the information in the story on page 92.
Use your own ideas too.

1 **Write Harry Day's recount of the fire.**

What did he hear first?   What did he see?   What did his dad do?   What happened next?

Remember! Write in the first person, like this:

First I heard a loud bang. I looked out of the window and I saw . . .

2 **Write the newspaper report of the fire at Mr Green's factory.**

Where was the fire? When did it start? How did it start? Who went to help? What did they do?
Remember the parts of a newspaper report:

> a headline   a first short paragraph   a photograph and caption   the rest of the report

Remember to include some direct speech.
What did these people say?

the fireman   policeman   Mr Green   Harry Day

3 **Write the TV reporter's interview with Mr Green.**

Think of questions the reporter can ask.   Think of Mr Green's answers.
Add to the questions below.   Make up new information.

What was in the factory?

There were …

How long have you
owned the factory?

I have owned it …

Project 5: The job that I would like

Write about a job that you would like to do.
Look at the pictures. Think about a job. Read the notes. Write four paragraphs.

1 Say what the job is.

I would like to be a . . .

2 Explain why you would like to the job. Say what things do you like doing.

I would like to do this job because I like working with . . .

enjoy doing . . .   I'm interested in . . .

3 Explain what a person with this job does.

Where does he or she work? Explain all the tasks in the job.

4 Find out about a person who does this job now.

Where does the person work? Why does he or she like the job?
Has anything special happened?
Write about the person.

or

Write about a famous person who did this job in the past.

Where and when did he or she work? Did anything special happen?
Why is the person famous?

5 Illustrate your writing.

Find pictures or draw pictures of people doing this job. Write captions.

Project 6: A biography

1 Think of a famous person from the past.

The person could be from

the ancient past

a long time ago

not very long ago

Choose somebody who interests you.

The person could be a man or a woman who

was important

was very brave

discovered something

helped other people

did something amazing

invented something

2 Find out facts about the person. Write the facts in order.

- Start with what the person did as a young boy or girl.
- Say what the person did as an adult.
- Say what happened at the end of the person's life.

3 Find or draw pictures to illustrate your biography.

Macmillan Education
Between Towns Road, Oxford, OX4 3PP
A division of Macmillan Publishers Limited
Companies and representatives throughout the world

ISBN: 978-0-230-02463-2

Designed by Anthony Godber
Illustrated by Beth Aulton, Katy Jackson, Chantal Kees, Dave Lowe, Hattie Newman, Philip Pepper,
Studio Pulsar, Gary Rees, Mark Ruffle, Martin Sanders, Barbara Vagnozzi, Joe Wilkins
Typeset by Wild Apple Design
Cover design by Oliver Design

The publishers would like to thank the following for their participation in the development of this course:
In Egypt – Ali Abdel Wahab, Christine Abu Sitta, Inas Agiz, Salma Ahmed, Hekmat Aly, Suzi Balaban,
Mohamed Eid, Bronwen El Kholy, Mostafa El Makhzangy, Hala Fouad, Jonathan French, Hisham
Howeedy, Saber Lamey, Nashaat Nageeb Gendy, Heidi Omara, Maha Radwan, Amany Shawkey,
In Russia – Tatiana Antonova, Elena Belonozhkina, Galina Dragunova, Irina Filonenko, Marina Gaisina,
Maria Goretaya, Oksana Guzhnovskaya, Irina Kalinina, Olga Kligerman, Galina Kornikova, Lidia
Kosterina, Sergey Kozlov, Irina Larionova, Irina Lenchenko, Irina Lyubimova, Karine Makhmuryan, Maria
Pankina, Anna Petrenkova, Elena Plisko, Natalia Vashchenko, Angelika Vladyko

The authors and publishers would like to thank the following for permission to reproduce their photographic
material:
Alamy/ Christophe Diesel-Michot p77(br), Alamy/ Werner Dieterich p36, Alamy/ Freefall Images p82(br),
Alamy/ Tom Hanley p54(b), Alamy/ Imagebroker p120(t), Alamy/ Pictures Colour Library p93(br), Alamy/
Picture Contact p143(cr), Alamy/ QA Photos p46(r), Alamy/ Qcumber p76, Alamy/ David Robertson
p40, Alamy/ Jeff Rotman p105(tl), Alamy/ David Seawell p103(r), Alamy/ Amoret Tanner p113, Alamy/
David Tipling p82(tl); **Alaska State Library**/ Claus Rodine Manuscript Collection p120(bl); **Ancient Art
and Architecture Collection Library**/ p129(t); **Arcaid**/ Bhaswaran Bhattacharya p41(b); Ardea/ Becca
Saunders p95(b); **Associated Press**/ p84(tl); **Bananastock**/ pp134(tr), 143(ct); **Brand X**/ p134(tl); **Corbis**/
Atlantide Phototravel p49, Corbis/ Dave Bartruff p48(c), Corbis/ Ralph A. Clevenger p105(tr), Corbis/ Jim
Craigmyle p82(cb), Corbis/ Fridmar Damm p43, Corbis/ Design Pics p41(t), Corbis/ Dex Image p143(br),
Corbis/ Dimitri Iundt p85, Corbis/ Andy Rain p46(l), Corbis/ Value Art p48(t), Corbis/ Brian A Vikander
p41(c), Corbis/ Ralph White p103(l); **Getty**/ pp54(tr), 84(tr), Getty/ Winston Davidian p93(ct), Getty/
David de Lossy p77(tl), Getty/ Shaun Egan p31, Getty/ Karen Moskowitz pp77(bl), 82(bl), Getty/ National
Geographic pp102, Getty/ Stock4B p54(c), Getty/ Stuart Westmorland p100; **Nature Picture Library**/
Jurgen Freund p95(t), Nature Picture Library/ David Shale p94; **NHPA**/ Photoshot p108; **Photolibrary**/
Doug Traverso p54(tl); **Photoshot**/ p56; **Press Association Photos**/ David Jones p84(cr); **Rex Features**/
Mike Kipling/ The Travel Library p77(tr); **Robert Harding World Imagery**/ Peter Richardson p30; **The
Ronald Grant Archive**/ Miramax Films p84(l); **Topfoto**/ Novosti p48(c & r insert).

Commissioned photographs by Clark Wiseman/www.studio-8.co.uk/ p 26, 34, 44, 52, 62, 70, 80, 84, 87, 88,
98, 106, 116, 124.

Printed and bound in Malaysia

2013   2012   2011
10 9 8 7 6 5 4 3 2